LIVINGSTON
The Making of a Scottish New Town

Elspeth M Wills

THE
RUTLAND
PRESS

Make it in Livingston

© Livingston Development Corporation

While every effort has been made to ensure that the material contained in this book is correct at the time of publication, neither the Corporation nor its agents take responsibility for any unintentional inaccuracies herein.

Cover design: Dorothy Steedman, Almond Design
Index: Anne O'Connor

Published by
The Rutland Press
for
Livingston Development Corporation
1996

ISBN 1 873 190 46 8

Cover photograph: Livingston Town Centre by Douglas Corrance
Sketches by David Anthony, Anthony Kerr Partnership
Design and typesetting: Almond Design, Edinburgh
Printed by Pillans & Wilson Greenaway, Edinburgh

CONTENTS

Introduction   1

A PLACE ON A MAP OF THE FUTURE

1. A Place in Time   3
2. The Place of New Towns   9
3. Deciding on a New Town   17
4. The First Days   23
5. The Master Plan   27

PEOPLE WORK AND PLACE

6. A Place for People   35
7. Make it in Livingston   41
8. A New House in a New Town   58
9. Down Your Way   68

THE HEART AND LIFEBLOOD OF THE TOWN

10. Building a Community   77
11. Thirty Years of Fun and Games   88
12. Fitting the Pieces Together   95
13. Almondvale – Heart of the Town   106

NO LONGER A NEW TOWN

14. New Town to Home Town   115
15. An End and a Beginning   121

APPENDICES

Board Members and Directors   122
Credits   123
Bibliography   125

Index   127

INTRODUCING LIVINGSTON

"Livingston Development Corporation will undertake to make Livingston a self contained vital and happy community of some 100,000 people enjoying all that is best of gracious living." This was how Sir David Lowe, the Chairman, summed up the immense task ahead in creating Scotland's fourth new town, in the Corporation's first annual report to the Secretary of State for Scotland in 1963. Some thirty three years later, Robert Watt ended his Chairman's Introduction to the Corporation's last annual report with the words "We are confident that we are leaving Livingston in a very healthy state and that, in general, the future is bright for residents and companies alike."

Thirty four years is a very short time in which to make a new community. During the intervening years, the rolling countryside of West Lothian was to witness the growth of a town with over 45,000 inhabitants and close on a thousand employers. The valley of the River Almond was to become the capital of Silicon Glen and the site of the second largest town in the Lothians. The name of local farms and country estates would acquire a very different meaning in Howden and Newyearfield. The small communities of Livingston Village and Livingston Station would be absorbed as Kirkton and Deans in the town to which they gave their name.

People would come to make a new life in Livingston from Glasgow and Galashiels, from the nearby mining communities and from Scotland's capital. Companies would come to make it in Livingston from as far afield as Texas and Tokyo. They would produce steel forgings and semiconductor wafers, software and shortbread, and in so doing would help to put Livingston's name on the world map.

Together they made Livingston one of Scotland's growth points and created more than 30,000 new jobs for Scotland. The people who worked for them found not only a new job but a new home and a new life. Many of these people helped to make a community with its clubs and cultural activities, and most important of all, with its own distinctive identity and voice.

Livingston's voice may not always have been in accord with that of its Development Corporation, the organisation charged in 1962 with building the new town, although relationships between the town and its creator were generally constructive. "Why aren't there more shops? There's nothing for young people to do at night. Why can't we have a better bus service?" were questions regularly asked in Forum, the community voice of the earliest residents, and the Community Councils, questions which served to spur the Development Corporation to further effort.

There was feeling as well as experience in the voice of the Corporation's second general manager, S E M Wright, when he said: "In a new town, the first five years are a hard slog, from five to ten years things gain momentum and after ten years, the heart develops and the momentum continues." This short account of the history of the first thirty four years of Livingston new town, and of the role of Livingston

Development Corporation within it, sets out to describe that slog, to record the momentum and look into the heart of the town as it developed.

It celebrates some of the town's achievements, Kirkton Campus and NEC, the Ecumenical Experiment and Scotland's first community schools. It looks back at some of the town's celebrations from the handing over of the key to the first Corporation house to the visit from the Queen to mark Livingston's Silver Jubilee. It also tells of a few of the darker moments; the aftermath of the great gale of 1968 or the effects of the closure of British Leyland's Bathgate plant on the town. What more than anything it records is how the task of making the town of Livingston was accomplished; the achievements, the opportunities, the setbacks.

Inevitably, in the attempt to describe the development of a town in a hundred pages commissioned in the last months of the Corporation's lifetime, of necessity, I have had to leave out much more than I have put in. It can be at most an overview touching only the surface of the events and personalities, the triumphs and frustrations which shaped Livingston's story.

I should like to take this opportunity of thanking Livingston Development Corporation for inviting me to write this account of the last thirty four years and in particular, Paul Filipek, Head of Planning and Landscape, for the hours spent in explaining the background to some of the events and for keeping me straight when I confused Dedridge with Deans. Without the unique contribution of the few staff and community leaders whom it was possible to interview in the time, the Corporation's Board minutes and policy statements would not have come alive. I should also like to acknowledge the co-operation of the Planning Exchange in giving me access to three interviews conducted with the Corporation's chief planners.

The future history of Livingston is in the making. For the errors and omissions in recording the past, I can only apologise while any views expressed are my own.

·A PLACE ON A MAP OF THE FUTURE·

1
·A PLACE IN TIME·

The River Almond rises at Hirst Hill near Shotts in Lanarkshire and over 25 miles later enters the Forth estuary at Cramond on the western outskirts of Edinburgh. Roughly half way on its journey to the sea, the Almond flows through a gentle valley which it has carved for itself among the undulating West Lothian hills. Until 1962, this valley had remained undisturbed for many centuries, witnessing the gradual evolution of farming patterns and the even tenor of agricultural life. From the 1860s onwards, dramatic changes took place on its periphery but in the valley itself, little was disturbed. From 1962, this valley became the heart of the new town of Livingston.

FOSSILS AND FARMS

At one point in geological time, the Almond flowed under the site of what was to become Livingston. Long before then, the area was part of a vast sub-tropical lake which covered most of East Central Scotland. As the lake silted up, rotting vegetation and sand gradually formed shales, limestone and sandstone which were then squeezed horizontally into a series of waves and troughs. As the earth moved and created new faults, outcrops of these deposits were brought to the surface. This geological activity laid down the mineral deposits which turned the environs of Livingston from a scattering of farms into the site of the world's first oil industry.

More recent geological events laid the foundations for the area's economy in the centuries before the discovery in the 1850s that its shale deposits yielded unexpected wealth. The contours of the landscape were rounded by the retreating glaciers of the Ice Age some 60,000 years ago. When the melting ice deposited a thick layer of boulder clay, the River Almond had to carve out a new course. providing fertile agricultural land on the valley floor as well as the means to eke out a reasonable living in the rougher pastures on the hills above. A combination of farming and shale mining provided a means of earning a living for the inhabitants of the three small communities, Bellsquarry, Livingston Station and Livingston Village, which were to become part of Livingston new town in 1962.

The immediate landscape shaped the design of the new town. Livingston is intersected from west to east by the shallow valley made by the Almond as it meanders on its three mile course through the town. To the south east is the gorge of the Murieston Water. Several tributaries including the Folly and Killandean Burns have carved out steep, wooded valleys on their way to join the Almond within the town itself. Two miles to the north, the basalt outcrop of Dechmont Law rises to a height of 711 feet, providing a natural backdrop to the town. To the south, the land slopes gently upwards to a height of around 600 feet above sea level.

LIVINGSTON ACQUIRES A NAME

Three Bronze Age burial mounds to the South of the Almond may be the first evidence of human habitation in the area. The creation of the first

The Earliest Resident
Lizzie, the world's oldest landliving amphibian is a relative of Eldeceeon, Livingston's earliest known resident. Both were discovered by Stan Wood, Scotland's leading fossil collector, in local shale beds. The Corporation was the first organisation of its kind to have a fossil named after it, commemorating its contribution towards Eldeceeon's purchase for the nation in 1986.

Mill to Heritage Centre
Eight years after a band of volunteers formed the Livingston Mill Restoration Group in 1967, the water wheel turned once more. In 1987, the Queen opened Livingston Mill Farm, restored with Corporation and MSC support. Ben, a retired milk horse became a firm favourite The Almond Valley Heritage Centre's attractions include a shale oil museum, a farm machinery collection, an interactive computer display and a nature trail.

significant settlement dates back to around 1120 when a Flemish nobleman, de Leving, established his "villa Leving" in the Almond valley. In order to defend his new domain, de Leving built a tower surrounded by a high wooden fence or peel close to a ford on the Almond. The presence of a powerful overlord demanded servants, farm workers and craftsmen, Livingston's first established residents. In 1991, the fortifications were reconstructed by the Corporation as the centrepiece of Peel Park.

Livingston soon attracted royal attention. A hunting lodge once stood on the site of Newyearfield farm, which takes its name from the time of year when the King customarily performed the ceremony of the Royal Touch. At the time it was believed that he had the power to cure scrofula, a form of TB, by sprinkling sufferers with holy water. In the Middle Ages, the area's water seems to have been reputed for its healing powers, with one well being dedicated to the Virgin Lady. It may have been christened Ladywell by the Knights Templar or Knights of St John, the medical and military order which had its Scottish headquarters in nearby Torphichen. The Knights owned land stretching up to the ridge of Dechmont Law.

Over the centuries as more peaceful times prevailed, country houses and farms replaced fortified keeps. The ford was now a crossing point for herds of cattle as they made their way south from the cattle fairs of Falkirk and Larbert. In 1764, the stone, two arched Howden Bridge was built to carry the Glasgow–Edinburgh turnpike road over the Almond.

By the mid 19th century, there were at least thirteen landowners in the area. The open views and healthy breezes attracted the first commuters including Edinburgh bankers and lawyers. Among the owners of the now vanished Charlesfield House, was the son of Henry Raeburn, one of Scotland's greatest portrait painters while Livingston Place and its purpose built kennels was a centre of the local hunt in the late 18th century. Amid the modern architecture of Livingston, three of these country houses, Alderstone, Bankton and Howden, and several farmsteads have found a new purpose as an office, a hotel and as an arts and community space.

Before the advent of steam, water was used to power industry and a number of mills were built alongside the Almond, including the New Calder Mills, one of Scotland's earliest paper mills and still in production. Upstream, Livingston Mill ground the grain of the local farming community.

Situated on the Glasgow–Edinburgh turnpike road, Livingston Village evolved as the hub of the local community. Its centre was the parish church, built in 1732 on the site of a previous building and remodelled in 1837. Its graveyard provides a continuity with the past. The farmers and tradesmen buried there would still recognise the immediate surroundings of the Livingston Inn and the stone bridge across the Almond although what they would make of the rest of the town is more difficult to imagine.

A separate village had grown up along the Edinburgh-Kilmarnock road taking its name, Bellsquarry from the local limestone quarry, operated by a Mr Bell. Village life revolved round the Elm Tree Inn, which remains to this day. In the early 19th century, the Inn also served as a stopping point for weary horses and thirsty passengers on their day-long journey between the two centres.

SIR PARAFFINE

In 1850, the even tenor of rural ways in the Almond Valley was unruffled by an event which was to change the life of the community for ever. In that year, James Young, a Glasgow chemist, patented his process for extracting oil from cannel coal sent to him by a friend from a mine at Boghead near Bathgate. It was known as cannel coal because it burned so brightly that local miners used a lump of it as a candle to read by.

With great speed and secrecy, Young opened the world's first oil refinery, surrounded by a high wall, at Whiteside on the outskirts of Bathgate. The market for the products from Young's oil was insatiable as until then, much of the world had to rely for lighting and lubrication on the evil smelling tallow, rendered from animal fat, or on expensive and increasingly scarce whale oil.

As the supply of cannel coal diminished, Young turned his attention to the local oil shales, securing some of the best seams for himself before his patent ran out in 1864. He built his new works, Young's Paraffin Light and Mineral Oil Company, on top of the vast deposits which ran from Seafield to Pumpherston, under the site of what today is Livingston. The foundation stone of the factory was

What's in a Name?
Livingston is called after the Flemish noble, de Leving whose son Thurston witnessed a charter of David I granting the church of "villa Leving" to the monks of Holyrood. As late as 1683, Livingston Kirk was referred to as Levingston whereas in the 18th century the village was known as Kirkton of Livingstone.

Livingstone's Last Days
A student friend of James "Paraffin" Young, David Livingstone, the explorer and missionary, laid the foundation stone of Young's refinery at Addiewell. Young remained deeply involved in his friend's fortunes, mounting a search party when Livingstone went missing and paying for two of his African servants to be brought to Britain after his death. A tree planted by Livingstone in the grounds of Young's home at Limefield, West Calder survives and the dam across the stream recalls Livingstone's recreation of the Victoria Falls. Long since vanished however, is the model of the thatched hut in which he died.

laid by David Livingstone, the African explorer and missionary, a friend of Young's from night school days.

RED GOLD

The expiry of Young's patent allowed others to exploit his process and the rush for oil was on. Oil mania changed the face of the local landscape. Within a year, over a hundred works sprang up to exploit the shales and cannel coal. At its height, over three million tons of oil shales a year were extracted from the mines, with the residues forming the vast, pink bings which dominated the landscape for many years. Over 40,000 people worked in the mines or in the factories, established alongside, manufacturing everything from candles to aviation fuel. In the 1930s, Scotland even had its own brand of petrol, "Scotch".

New villages sprang up almost overnight to accommodate the miners and factory workers. One of these was Livingston Station, taking its name from the passenger halt opened in 1849 on the Edinburgh-Bathgate railway. The presence of the railway proved attractive to one of Young's rivals, the West Lothian Oil Co, which opened the Deans Crude Oil Works in 1884. In the next year, the company built sixteen cottages, known as the Deans Row, to house its workers. Although the works soon proved uneconomic, they were modernised and reopened in 1897 by the Pumpherston Oil Company. A number of new mines were opened to feed the retorts of the Deans works with its ever growing shale bing. The famous Pumpherston seam was mined at Alderstone and an overhead railway carried shale from the Dedridge mine to the Oakbank refinery. Some of the first residents of Livingston new town spent their working lives hundreds of feet underground in the dark and potentially dangerous tunnels of the mines.

LIVINGSTON STATION "NEW TOWN"

As more mines were dug and the Deans works expanded, Deans Row rapidly became Livingston Station. Some of its 2,000 inhabitants at the turn of the century had emigrated from Ireland, looking for work and a better future in the Scottish mines. Others may have come from the Scottish fishing villages whose livelihood was threatened by the declining herring shoals, providing a possible explanation of Fisherrow on Main Street.

The Deans Oil Company which essentially owned the village prided itself on the high standard of accommodation offered to its workers, compared with the traditional coal mining villages of Lanarkshire. It wished its houses to be referred to as cottages rather than rows. Each brick built cottage consisted of at least a livingroom and kitchen, both with box beds, and a scullery. At first, the cottages did not have piped water and housewives had to draw their supplies for cooking, washing and the endless baths, the first priority for a miner coming off shift, from a standpipe in the street. The rows had a tiny strip of garden fronting the street and a drying area at the back.

From 1904, shopping revolved round the "Store", a branch of the West Calder Co-operative Society. The Co-op sold most day-to-day necessities, with the added bonus of a "divi" or share of the profits at the end of the month. Mobile vans from the Calders and Broxburn also made their rounds of the village.

At first, infants were taught in temporary accommodation in the village hall, while older children walked to the school in Livingston Village until a purpose-built school was opened in 1908. Only seven years later, an additional four classrooms and a cookery and woodwork room were required. The school roll increased again from a more unexpected source in 1941 when 74 evacuees and their teachers arrived from Greenock in the midst of the Blitz.

Like many mining villages, Livingston Station was a traditional, tightly knit community. Breeding and racing whippets, greyhounds and pigeons were popular pastimes as was quoits, played by throwing horseshoes at a target set in a special area of grass. The bowling greens attached to the Deans Institute produced several international class players, while the football team was the starting point for the young hopefuls of the village, two of whom, Jimmy Scoular and Tommy Walker went on to careers in top division football as captain of Newcastle United and as manager of Heart of Midlothian FC.

As the century progressed, the Lothian shale industry slipped into slow but terminal decline, overtaken by cheap oil imports from the Middle East. By the mid 1930s, the industry was reduced to the central refinery at Pumpherston, served by five crude oil works and thirteen mines. Although the Deans Works shut down in 1949, the last refinery did not close until 1964, the year in which the new town's first factory opened.

In its day and on a much less ambitious scale, Livingston Station was a new town, sharing many of the characteristics and challenges which were to become familiar with the creation of its successor, Livingston. From the 1880s, Livingston Station too went through a period of rapid expansion, drawing its residents from far and wide to seek employment in a new industry. It had its Church, school and community centre in the Deans Institute, all of which were to play a vital part in the early days of the next new town.

An Insatiable Appetite

The Deans Oil Works' retorts consumed 1,000 tons of shale a day. When mined, the shale was slate blue but as the oil was extracted in the retort, it turned pink, then red. According to one Livingston miner, "It was just like roasting a bit of cheese for your supper. Just as gravy flows as the cheese bubbles on the toast, so the crude oil oozed out".

New towns have always provoked strong reactions. In 1856, Lord Cockburn, the Edinburgh judge and conservationist wrote: "What a site did nature give us for our New Town! Yet, what insignificance in its plan! what poverty in all its details!"

2
·THE PLACE OF NEW TOWNS·

New towns are almost as old as towns themselves. Unlike other forms of urban settlement, however, they have been created from the outset to achieve a specific purpose rather than simply taking shape over the centuries. New towns have been established by pioneers to make their mark on virgin territory or by idealists as a means of expressing their vision of society. Landowners moved villages which spoilt the view from their new mansions and industrialists built towns in the country, beside the source of the raw materials or energy needed for their factories. More recently, the concept of new towns has been adopted by planners and policy makers to relieve the congestion of cities and create new centres of growth. Places as different as Alexandria, New Delhi and Washington DC were all at one time new towns.

LIVINGSTON'S SCOTTISH PEDIGREE

The proposal, for a new town at Livingston was thus part of a long tradition, in which Scotland had played a significant part. In the 18th and early 19th centuries alone, over two hundred new towns and villages were built in Scotland. Some like Inveraray and Kinross involved the transplantation of existing communities out of sight of the country seats of the Scottish aristocracy. Others were built to provide housing for workers in new or expanding industries, from fishing to textiles. In the 1780s, the Glasgow cotton magnate and pioneer of mass production, David Dale established a complex of mills at New Lanark, to benefit from the cheap source of power provided by the waterfalls of the Clyde. He appointed his future son in law, Robert Owen as manager of New Lanark, providing Owen with the unique opportunity to put into practice his ideas for a model industrial community, with its school, community centre and company shop.

It comes as a surprise to some visitors to Edinburgh that the New Town is not a modern suburb but one of Europe's most outstanding examples of 18th century town planning and architecture. Its grid plan of streets interspersed with gardens and its long rows of terraces in a fairly uniform style reveal its origins as a development which was created from the outset.

Edinburgh's New Town shares some of the features of modern new towns. Designed to a master plan by the architect James Craig, it was built on agricultural land, separated from the Old Town by the marshes of the Nor' Loch, which when drained became Princes Street Gardens. It was planned at a time of rapid population growth in response to the acute congestion and shortage of land within the capital. The exodus of the prosperous and the enterprising to more spacious and airy accommodation can be seen as an early form of overspill. There was, however, no place for industry in this particular vision.

Scotland's later 19th century new towns anticipated a different theme behind the development of their 20th century successors, that of economic growth. Small villages like Motherwell and Coatbridge grew into substantial towns on the back of coal mining and iron smelting. The tenements of Clydebank appeared almost overnight following the decision by the Glasgow shipbuilders, G & J Thomson, to move their yard down river, in order to meet market demand for ever larger and more powerful liners. The companies behind the rapid expansion of many of these towns, however, showed little heed for planning or for people. By the end of the 19th century, Coatbridge was "a desolate, black district of smoke, coal and ashes - treeless, sunless, the verdure of Nature's surface scarified and loaded with rubbish dumps."

EBENEEZER'S NEW TOWN

In the same year as the writer of Murray's Handbook for Scotland described many of Scotland's industrial towns in equally damning phrases, another author was at work on a book which was to introduce a concern for the environment into planning and inspire the development of the UK's 20th century new towns. The author was Ebeneezer Howard, born in 1850, who in his youth experienced the teeming life of the City of London, the tranquillity of the rural English towns and finally the pioneering spirit of Chicago. Known as the Garden City, over the previous twenty five years, Chicago had grown from a town of 12,000 people to a city of 307,000 inhabitants.

These very different experiences set Ebeneezer Howard on the ten year struggle to publish his radical rethinking of urban life. His solution to the 19th century dilemma of how to tackle urban overcrowding and rural depopulation was simple: "town and country must be married and out of this joyous union will spring a new hope, a new life, a new civilisation." 'Tomorrow: a Peaceful Path to Real Reform', reissued as 'Garden Cities of Tomorrow',

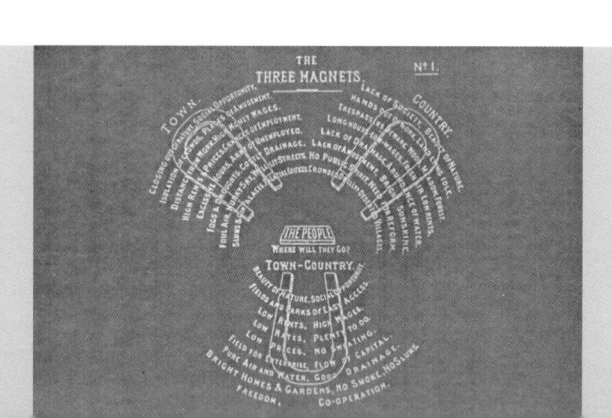

The Three Magnets
Ebeneezer Howard's drawing showing the benefits and drawbacks of living in the town or country and how they could be resolved through his Garden City concept has become the world's most famous town planning diagram. "I was led to put forward proposals ... to build by private enterprise, pervaded by public spirit, an entirely new town, industrial, residential and agricultural."

was not a theoretical treatise but a practical manual of how to set about creating a new town in the country.

Residents of the UK's congested cities would be encouraged to set up industrial colonies in the countryside, where they would be provided with work and housing. Profit from the ensuing increase in land values would be reinvested in the community, once the initial commitment to those financing the new venture was repaid. The town would be managed by a Central Council with similar powers to a local authority but because it was also the town's landlord, the freedom to decide the destiny of its creation. If Ebeneezer Howard were to visit Livingston today, he would feel on familiar ground.

Howard was a practical visionary, whose overriding aim was to put his ideas to the test. He quickly won over supporters for his ideas, forming the Garden City Association in 1899 and giving illustrated lectures throughout the country including Edinburgh to stimulate interest in his project. In 1903, he formed a company to raise money for the first Garden City, Letchworth in Hertfordshire and less than twenty years later, the second site at Welwyn was purchased.

In Letchworth, the creative partnership of Howard, and the young architects, Parker and Unwin, laid down many of the principles that were to guide the design of the new towns which followed. They made full use of the natural contours of the landscape, planting and conserving trees to enhance views or screen less desirable features. Houses were placed together in small groups, at low densities and with sunny open aspects. The first planners also experienced some of the tensions which would be felt in the later Development Corporations, notably the architects' desire to enforce high standards in the use of materials and the design of buildings against the commercial pressures to let sites, sometimes to tenants whose aspirations and priorities were very different.

With Howard's death in 1928, much of the impetus for Garden Cities was lost, although a small band of devoted followers struggled on with the development of Welwyn against huge financial odds. Also beset by financial constraints, most local authorities tackled the problem of overcrowded cities by building large estates on their periphery. Although not in the Scottish housing tradition of compact tenements with shared back courts, the influence of garden cities was felt in Scotland to a small extent during the 1920s, in the design of local authority housing estates such as Knightswood on the western outskirts of Glasgow. During the period, a start was made to a garden city planned by Parker and Unwin beside the naval dockyard at Rosyth but building was halted, with the mothballing of the dockyard in 1925.

LORD REITH'S VISION

The Second World War provided the immediate impetus for the new town movement, although the first step had already been taken in 1937 with the appointment of the Barlow Commission on the Geographical Distribution of the Industrial Population.

In the same year as War broke out, the Commission made its recommendation that the drift towards London and the major cities must be halted by the decentralisation of industry and population to garden cities, suburbs and satellite towns and to existing small towns and regional centres.

The War both accelerated the need for new towns and provided the framework to carry their planning forward. Bomb damage proved the final straw to an urban fabric, showing signs of strain for nearly a century. National planning and a strong central administration demonstrated that paradoxically, it was possible to improve the nation's health at a time of severe food shortages, and that people could be rehoused quickly and cheaply in the extremely popular "prefabs". The Beveridge Report which sold over half a million copies, not only ushered in the welfare state but struck a deep chord in the popular conscience. There was no going back to the bad old days of slums, poverty and poor working conditions.

In the dark days of the War, Winston Churchill appointed Lord Reith, the founder of the BBC, to be his Minister of Works with special responsibility for post-war reconstruction. Although he promptly sacked Reith from the post in 1942, the forceful and forthright Glaswegian soon resurfaced, this time as the Chairman of an inter-departmental New Towns Committee set up by the Labour Prime Minister Lord Attlee in 1945. Its brief was to look at the development of new towns as a response to urban congestion and to set out guidelines as to how they should be managed and resourced.

Under the characteristic efficiency and iron-will of its Chairman, the Committee produced three reports within the space of a few months, with most of its recommendations being adopted in the New Towns Act 1946 and the corresponding New Towns (Scotland) Act 1946. In developing the structure for the new towns, Lord Reith drew heavily on his own experience at the BBC. The new Development Corporations were to consist of a number of specialist departments, under the overall direction of a Board and General Manager.

Lord Reith's final report not only laid down the logic for new communities but set out in precise detail how they should be run. Contrary to Howard's original model, there was to be no place for private funding or community enterprise in the management of Reith's new towns, reflecting his strong belief in publicly financed, independently operated organisations. The towns were to be planned top-down rather than bottom-up although one place on each Board was reserved for a local person. One of Reith's recommendations which MPs rejected was that there should be only one local authority for the whole site of each new town. The early development of Livingston might have been considerably simpler if his advice had been heeded.

THE FIRST GENERATION
The time was right to create new towns. With its tidy approach to people as well as places, planning was gaining acceptance as a practical tool as well as an academic discipline. New towns fitted with the

It was an environment like this that decided many Glaswegians to start a new life in a new town.

thinking of most UK planners that population densities in cities should be reduced and that to avoid urban sprawl, cities should be given clear boundaries by surrounding them with Green Belts, on which most building was prohibited. Excess population should be moved out beyond these Green Belts to new or expanded towns.

Designers were longing to try out the ideas of the 1930's modern movement in architecture, the symbol of a brighter and better future. Having demonstrated during the War that good planning could win victories, officers now seeking a civilian career were seen as ideal candidates to manage new towns, a tradition which was to continue for many years. Livingston's first General Manager was a Brigadier while several of his Board and management team had distinguished military records.

In the space of five years, 14 new towns were established throughout the UK except Northern Ireland including two in Scotland. East Kilbride was designated in 1947 followed by Glenrothes in 1948. East Kilbride had been identified as the site for one of five new towns proposed for West Central Scotland in the Clyde Valley Regional Plan of 1946. The Plan was produced by the Government and 18 local authorities to guide the future of the region in the light of the crisis faced by Glasgow.

Investment in housing failed to keep pace with the rapid population and industrial growth which made Glasgow the "second city of the British Empire" by the end of the 19th century. Many of the industries on which the city's wealth was based such as shipbuilding and heavy engineering were now showing signs of economic distress due to declining markets and a failure to remain competitive in the face of technological advance.

War damage to Glasgow's housing stock was only the tip of the iceberg in a city which was the most densely populated in the UK. 700,000 people were packed into 1,800 acres of land. Over a third of the city's inhabitants lived in one or two room tenements, many of which lacked even the basic amenities of a bath or a separate WC. The 1951 Census revealed the scale of the problem, classifying 44% of households as overcrowded Although Glasgow Corporation had built a number of estates between the Wars, much of the housing remained in the hands of private landlords who were unable or unwilling to invest in bringing their property up to tolerable standards.

The Clyde Valley Regional Plan summed up

Glasgow's future: "large scale surgical treatment is now belatedly recognised to be the only possible solution" Half a million people would have to be moved out of the city in order to reduce housing densities and allow the slums to be rebuilt. Glasgow Corporation, however, thought differently. A mixture of civic pride and concern at the loss of rateable income resulted in the city pulling out of the Clyde Valley Plan and resolving to tackle its own problems within its own boundaries.

Starting with the notorious Gorbals, the Corporation established a total of 29 Comprehensive Development Areas where the solution would be to tear down everything and rebuild again from scratch. Over the next two decades, over 300 high rise blocks, many using new industrial building techniques, were to change the city's skyline before the programme was halted in the mid 1970s in favour of urban renewal.

Glasgow Corporation was faced with the immediate problem as to where to put people while their new homes were under construction. Even if the house building programme was completed, the lower housing densities achieved meant that there would be a shortfall between people and homes. With any attempts to encroach on the Green Belt strongly resisted by central Government, by the mid 1950s Glasgow was forced to admit that new towns were an inevitable component of the city's requirement for 100,000 houses outside the area.

Given an initial target population of no more than 50,000, East Kilbride, one of the five new towns envisaged in the Clyde Valley Regional Plan, could not cope alone with the planned exodus of people and industry from Glasgow. Cumbernauld was, therefore, designated in 1955 specifically to take some of Glasgow's overspill population. Glasgow Corporation made a financial contribution for every family accepted as a new town tenant.

The rationale for Scotland's second new town, Glenrothes, was a variation on the same theme, the need to move industry and people away from the declining centres of West Central Scotland. The immediate problem was the imminent exhaustion of the Lanarkshire coal field, coupled with the need for the skills of the resident miners to exploit huge, new seams of coal recently discovered in Fife. Glenrothes got off to a difficult start, as the Rothes coal mine which was to be the town's major employer, soon turned out to be unworkable.

After a period of uncertainty about this brave new experiment, new towns in Scotland, as in the UK as a whole, had become a central part of Government industrial, housing and social policy by the early 1960s. The progress of the first generation of new towns had been closely monitored and many lessons learned, notably the need to provide more than just a physical infrastructure in order to support a new and predominantly young community.

New towns had proved their ability not simply to deliver the intended redistribution of population but to attract new industries and encourage prosperity. Building new towns with a target population of at least 30,000 on green fields also provided a more

Oats and oil - Livingston around 1962

cost-effective and often less controversial solution than the other option, adopted in the 1950s, of expanding existing centres of population.

In successive Government reports, there was increasing mention of a new town for South East Scotland. In line with the shift in regional policy away from new towns as primarily a housing resource to acting as a focal point for growth, this new town was envisaged as the centre of a sub-regional economy of up to a quarter of a million people. In July, 1961, the Government announced that this new town was to be Livingston.

THE OTHER FOUR

Before looking in detail at how Livingston grew from three villages to a town of over 45,000 people in the space of thirty years, it is worth briefly touching on what happened to the new town movement as a whole in Scotland. Irvine, Scotland's fifth new town, was designated in 1966. Irvine was different again, in that it was designed to draw together a number of small conurbations in North Ayrshire to provide a focus for economic growth to the west of Glasgow.

Work started on a sixth new town, Stonehouse in Lanarkshire, in 1973 occasioned by a perceived continuing shortfall in West Central Scotland's housing stock and Scottish Office concern over the standards of the Glasgow redevelopment programme. Its existence was to be short lived. Its development was abruptly halted only three years later, in a climate of increasing doubt about population and economic growth articulated notably by the new Strathclyde Regional Council.

With hindsight, it is perhaps more remarkable that Stonehouse was ever given the green light than that it was wound up so quickly. By the end of the 1960s, overspill had largely lost its momentum although the programme was not formally concluded by the Secretary of State for Scotland until nearly a decade later. The 1971 Census revealed that no less than 25,000 people, mainly professionals and skilled workers, were leaving Glasgow every year, double the anticipated number. Overspill and the new towns were blamed for this situation, although in fact, together, they only accounted for a quarter of the exodus from the city. The new towns retaliated by arguing that on the contrary they helped to stem the flood of emigration from Scotland.

By the early 1970s, profound changes had taken place in the social and economic makeup of the UK. The post-War baby boom had been replaced by a sharp decline in the birth rate. Family sizes were becoming smaller and increasingly, women expected to combine marriage with a job, often out of economic necessity. Recession in the early 1970s brought fear of a return to the dole queues of the 1930s. Glasgow was not alone among the older cities in claiming that the new towns were drawing away all their industries. The stark fact soon emerged, however, that these businesses had not moved but died.

In the light of these changes, both national and local government needed to develop a new response very rapidly to the problems of the inner cities. This reassessment was marked formally in 1976 by an announcement from the Secretary of State for the Environment that in England and Wales resources in future would be directed to the inner cities and that the role of new towns would be reappraised. Although the Scottish Office maintained an independent stance, this speech marked the turning point both in funding and policy away from the new towns towards the regeneration of the older economic centres and in Scotland's case towards tackling the problems of the peripheral estates. Continuing recessions, a change of Government in 1979 and increasingly severe restraints on public spending, as well as a radical rethinking of the role of cities, confirmed or brought forward the date for winding up the individual Development Corporations. Livingston was among the very last to go.

A Beginning and an End
The Scotsman headline, "Livingston will get its first tenants in 1964", had an added urgency, if not irony. Less than a fortnight before, the West Lothian Courier carried a very different headline: "the Final Blow." The closure of the BP refinery complex with the loss of 1,050 jobs effectively ended the shale oil century although one refinery was to remain in production for another couple of years, using imported shales.

The Village Pump
The milk boy is not the only reminder of the 1950s. The Livingston Village pump was a meeting place as some of the older houses did not have piped water, gas or electricity and were lit by paraffin oil. There was also no mains sewerage.

3 · DECIDING ON A NEW TOWN ·

Although Livingston formally came into being on 17th April, 1962, the concept of a new town in the Lothians had been mooted as early as 1948, when Sir Frank Mears reported to the Central and South-East Scotland Regional Planning Advisory Committee on the future development of the region's economy. In his report, he described a series of "constellations" to act as focal points for growth. One of these was located west of Edinburgh, close to the Calders.

During the 1950s, there was a gradual shift in the thinking of economists and planners away from the immediate post-War policy of tackling the problems of areas with high unemployment to encouraging areas of growth. Increasing dissatisfaction with the limitations of simply propping up declining areas led to the establishment by the Scottish Council Development and Industry of an influential committee of industrial, education and government leaders under the chairmanship of J N Toothill of Ferranti Ltd to find a way forward. Its Inquiry into the Scottish Economy 1960-1 was a landmark document, which essentially marked the watershed from rescue areas to growth areas.

The Government swiftly responded with a review of how the latter might be achieved, setting out its policy for implementation in the White Paper, "Central Scotland a Programme for Development and Growth." Although this was not laid before Parliament until November 1963, the same month as Livingston produced its own Master Plan, the review influenced the proposals for designating the new town. It recommended strengthening the role of central Government in regional development and broke new ground by bringing together economic and physical planning. A new concept was introduced of "growth areas", chosen for their potential advantages as locations for industrial expansion. Greater Livingston was confirmed as one of the eight growth areas in Central Scotland.

CHOOSING THE SITE

On 4th July, 1961, Livingston was conceived, when J S Maclay, Secretary of State for Scotland announced to the Scottish Grand Committee that a site to the west of Edinburgh was to be found for the building of Scotland's fourth new town. A site "in or near the Calders" won the day over Lugton in Ayrshire.

Guidelines were prepared for the selection of the site. Level and stable ground was required for building, in practice a major problem as much of West Lothian was hilly or riddled with old mineworkings. Given the widely held view in the 1960s that an industrial town needed a population of 50-70,000 in order to have a sufficient pool of labour, the site had to accommodate a population of up to 70,000 people. "Good communications were important as well as a range of factories", if new industries were to be attracted to the area.

The site of Livingston was one of the few places away from the congested Clyde Valley which satisfied these conditions. The area on which the new town was to be built lay 15 miles to the west of Edinburgh, Scotland's capital and 29 miles east of Glasgow, the country's main industrial and commercial centre. Sixteen miles to the north west was the port of Grangemouth. The boundaries were skirted by two railway lines and close to possible lines for a proposed motorway between Edinburgh and Glasgow.

Livingston allowed the simultaneous tackling of two constraints to the growth of the Central Scotland economy: the housing crisis faced by Glasgow and the industrial dereliction left by the local mining industry. The legacy of coal and shale oil mining was all too visible in the bings and spoil heaps which created an almost lunar landscape in parts of West Lothian. Small villages which had sprung up alongside the mines and chemical factories had lost their raison d'être when the industries closed. The mine and factory owners had little regard for their surroundings. When times were good, they gobbled up the agricultural land but when the industry finally went into terminal decline in the 1950s, they abandoned crumbling buildings and rusting machinery to the elements. The sheer unattractiveness of the environment was a major deterrent to new industries moving in.

THE THREE VILLAGES

The area which was to be designated as Livingston in 1962 contained a number of farms and three small communities which together had a population of around 2,000 people. Livingston Village consisted of little more than a scattering of houses round the Church and Inn. At one time, there had been three churches and briefly even a prisoner of war camp in a series of grey huts erected in a field opposite Bloom Farm.

The Village still had a Post Office which doubled as a general grocery although earlier in the century, the

The Deans Institute

Community life in the oil company village of Livingston Station centred on the Deans Institute. Its hall which could seat 500 was used for concerts, whist drives, dances, wedding receptions, Guides and Scouts, political meetings and badminton. Off it were separate committee rooms for men and women and at the rear, a billiard room, a games room and a "quiet room" with newspapers. The Institute was managed by a committee drawn from the local community without whose permission no meeting could be held.

The Elm Tree Inn
The hamlet of Bellsquarry, whose local stone was used in the National Monument on Edinburgh's Calton Hill, was included in the designated area which "could accommodate an interesting and compact town of 70,000 persons in conditions of high amenity."
Draft New Town Designation Order, 1962

community supported several stores and a fish and chip shop, as well as a joiner's and a blacksmith's forge. In the 1920s, the Post Office had also been the headquarters of one of Scotland's more unusual industries, the production of comic postcards. It was run by the post-mistress's husband Robert Braid who used local scenes as the background for many of his postcards and even persuaded some of the villagers to be photographed in fancy dress.

At the south west corner of the designated area was Bellsquarry with its inn and row of traditional Council houses and to the north was the largest of the three villages, Livingston Station. With the closure of the Deans Oil Works at the end of the Second World War, some of the heart went out of Livingston Station. A start was made to pull down the old miners' rows and replace them with modern Council houses. One dramatic change occurred in 1955, when residents voted to end the village's status as a "dry" area and Rab's Bar opened for business. The next year, passenger trains ceased to stop at the Halt.

The village still had several shops, a primary school and a part-time doctor's surgery. Older children had to travel to school in Bathgate. The Deans Institute was the centre of community life doubling up on a Sunday as the Roman Catholic Church. Pigeon racing, bowling and angling were popular sports, as was cheering on Livingston United Football Club to victory in the Scottish Secondary Juveniles league.

Although rumours abounded, the villagers first discovered formally that they were about to become new town residents in January, 1962, when a map showing the proposed boundaries of Livingston was pinned up in the Livingston Village Post Office. Louis Meiklejohn, the headmaster of Livingston Station primary school wrote in his log book: "it would appear that this village is included as well as Old Livingston."

A START TO NEGOTIATIONS

Once the 6,692 acre site had been chosen, there was much to do behind the scenes. A small team of Scottish Office civil servants masterminded the operation. Negotiations were entered into with the local landowners and farmers to start the process of purchasing sites for the future town. Livingston was fortunate in that much of the designated area was owned by a member of the Scottish aristocracy, the Earl of Rosebery who was prepared to sell his land.

Lengthy consultations took place with local authorities and other organisations which would be expected to provide everything from water and electricity to schools, playing fields and health services. In 1962, local government was carried out primarily by County Councils, with a large number of District Councils based on one or two small towns and villages being responsible for amenities like recreation. Livingston was the only Scottish new town area to be split between two County Councils; 3,350 acres being in Midlothian County and the remaining 3,342 in West Lothian County.

To further complicate the planning of the new town, the area fell within the jurisdiction of no less than five District Councils; East Calder and a corner of West Calder in Midlothian and Bathgate and Torphichen, Livingston and Whitburn, and Uphall in West Lothian. Each District had different priorities and budget constraints, which were to result on occasions in delays and protracted negotiations before Livingston could acquire the open spaces and sports facilities that would be essential to bind together the fast growing community.

DESIGNATING LIVINGSTON

On 15th January, 1962, the Secretary of State for Scotland announced his plans for Livingston, giving a month for objectors to prepare their case. Normally, when the detailed plans for a new town were published, a number of objections were raised from farmers concerned at the loss of income, residents reluctant to sacrifice amenity and local authorities concerned about the burden on the rates. Livingston was the only new town in the UK to be designated without a public inquiry. This may be seen as a tribute to the skill of the negotiators although the unique No Profit No Loss agreement, an incentive offered to the local authorities, was to complicate the Corporation's finances for many years.

The Draft New Town (Livingston) Designation Order set the ground rules for the new town. Although policy was rapidly moving towards the new concept of growth centres, to be articulated in the White Paper only a year later, the Designation Order gave the housing of Glasgow's overspill population as the main reason for establishing a fourth new town. It acknowledged, however, the opportunity presented by Livingston to "use overspill constructively to create a new focus of industrial activity in Central Scotland" and to provide a link between the expansion round the Forth estuary and the economic problems of the West.

One of the site's advantages was its proximity to

Miners to Assembly Workers
Some ex-shale workers found work on the new Houstoun Industrial Estate while others were employed in the BMC tractor plant.. At first they found it difficult to adapt to the new working conditions, standing for hours on end on an assembly line alongside people from all over Scotland. Writing in 1965, Rev David Torrance, the Minister of Livingston parish, wrote "Now the majority, with lighter work, cleaner and safer working conditions and higher wages, speak appreciatively of the change." One of the perks of working for BMC was the ability to buy a car at a reduced rate.

Greetings from Livingston
"The Village Blacksmith", "Coming through the Rye" and "the Sweep and the Washing" were among the most popular postcard titles developed by Robert Braid, in his dark room below Livingston Village Post Office.. The door on which he displayed his works of art was preserved when the shop was modernised. As a way of encouraging visitors to the town, in 1972 the Corporation issued a set of two coloured postcards, of Howden House and children playing in Ladywell, which were sold in local shops, the Howden Park Centre and Scottish Tourist Board offices.

the road and rail network, with the proposed new stretch of the A8 trunk road between Edinburgh and Glasgow envisaged as running through the town south of Dechmont Law. Factories could line the new road, as well as being accommodated on an industrial estate in the north east of the town. The Draft Order stressed the attractions of the landscape, envisaging that "this pleasant environment might attract a large component of private building." Although energy supplies would be relatively easy to bring into the town, water and sewerage would present immediate problems although both issues were already being addressed by the relevant authorities.

Given concerns about the loss of valuable farm land, which had delayed the designation of other Scottish new towns, the Order devoted a considerable amount of space to reassuring farmers of the proposed procedures to purchase land and minimise disruption. The limits of the town largely followed the boundaries of existing farms to avoid splitting them and efforts were to be made to keep farms in production until the land was needed for development. This resulted in several early residents of the town finding sheep on their doorstep or being plagued by swarms of insects at harvest time.

The terms of the No Profit No Loss agreement with the two County Councils were set out. In order not to place too high a burden on the rates, in the early years, the Corporation would assist in funding elements of the town's infrastructure such as roads normally the responsibility of the County Council. In return, ratepayers would not benefit from the increased income which would eventually accrue with rising land values. Instead, any surplus income would go towards repaying over a period of up to 60 years the Government loans which the new town's administration, Livingston Development Corporation would borrow in order to finance the development of the town. In line with Cumbernauld and many of the English new towns, the new Corporation was also to be effectively its own planning authority, with the granting of a Special Development Order.

The Draft Order also hinted at things to come, when it recommended that the two County Councils should jointly appoint a consultant "of the highest calibre" to examine the economy and social and physical fabric of West Lothian and the north west of Midlothian including proposals for tackling the area's derelict land and buildings. The Development Corporation would be given powers to assist with the removal of eyesores close to the town.

In summing up, the Draft Designation Order made clear for the first time how Livingston was to differ from other new towns. "A comprehensive regional plan would enable the new town and the various town development and overspill schemes around it to create a modern environment which would be attractive to industry and population alike, and competitive within the economy of Britain as a whole." In other worlds, Livingston was to be planned not as a self-contained community but as the centre for a much wider area.

THE FIRST DAY

With the Draft Designation Order being accepted without the need for a public inquiry, events moved quickly to a conclusion. A "shadow" Board had already been appointed by the Secretary of State and plans for the launch were put in hand. Although the statutory order establishing the Corporation which went under the unwieldy title of the New Town (Livingston) (Development Corporation) Order 1962 was not formally passed until 9th July, designation day was set as 17th April. A separate New Town (Livingston) Designation Order was passed setting out the physical area to be occupied by the new town.

A press launch was held in Howden House to mark the occasion. Next day, Livingston made the first of many front page headlines, with The Scotsman confidently predicting that "Livingston will Get its First Tenants in 1964." It was to be proved right.

Past and Future Witness

Howden House has many memories. It is associated with the family of Henry Raeburn, the eminent Scottish portrait painter. Dr Gregory, inventor of Gregory's Mixture, the panacea found in every Victorian nursery, was married here, while the house was later owned by James Stoddart who married "Paraffin "Young's daughter. Before the Corporation took it over, it belonged to the Ministry of Agriculture and Fisheries. Since 1962, the Queen, foreign diplomats, Japanese businessmen, the Chinese Premier, thespians and many local residents have journeyed up its drive.

A Crest with No Supporters
The town's crest is made up of the gillyflowers of the Earl of Livingston, the primrose of Lord Rosebery and a representation of the river Almond. Although the Board suggested supporters representing Glasgow and Edinburgh to symbolise the new town's role in linking Central Scotland,, the Lord Lyon turned down its request on the grounds that this would make Livingston appear subservient to the two cities or, even worse, a mere suburb of the capital. He also vetoed the proposed motto: "Yes we will" in response to the Earl of Livingston's "Si je peux".

4
THE FIRST DAYS

THE FIRST OF 447 BOARD MEETINGS

Immediately after the formal launch, the new Chairman, Sir David Lowe decided to call his first Board meeting. It was a distinguished gathering. As a well known and respected agriculturalist, Sir David's background was to come in useful when negotiating land with local farmers. The Deputy Chairman was William Taylor, a lawyer and Convenor of Glasgow Corporation's Planning Committee who took over as Chairman in 1965.

The two County Councils were represented by their Convenors, James Methven for Midlothian and Peter Walker for West Lothian. Rear Admiral Sir Peter Reid was joined by three leading members of the Scottish business community: John Rankin, Secretary of the Bank of Scotland, Sir William Sinclair, a former Director of the Dunlop rubber company and William Miller, the general manager of Rolls Royce in Scotland.

The Board's first agenda must have been its shortest. The Chairman instructed the civil servants in attendance, to set in motion the process to recruit the management team. They were also asked to draw up a list of items for the Board to consider at future meetings and to erect signs to mark the designated area.

THE FIRST RECRUITS

The first priority was to appoint staff. National advertising elicited a strong field of candidates drawn mainly from other new towns or local authorities. In June, the Board appointed Brigadier Arthur Purches as the new town's first General Manager, a post which he took up on 1st September, 1962. He soon got his feet under the desk, being on familiar territory as the General Manager of Glenrothes new town for the past four years. By the start of 1963, the team was in place with James Kelly, previously Town Clerk of Hamilton, as Secretary and Legal Adviser, Arnold Dalton, the Town Chamberlain of Clydebank as Chief Finance Officer and Peter Daniel, in the vital post of Chief Architect and Planning Officer.

The last post proved the most difficult to fill. One interviewee, from an English new town was somewhat startled to be offered the job at the end of the interview. He asked for more time to consult his family, eventually deciding against the move. The post was re-advertised at which point Peter Daniel applied. He had the unusual distinction of holding qualifications in architecture, planning and landscaping. Although with a building company at the time, he had previously worked on the design of an architecturally adventurous housing estate in Peterlee new town.

Once the senior management was in place, recruitment proceeded rapidly with 31 staff by March, 1963, the figure more than doubling to 85 during the next year. At its peak, in the late 1970s, the Corporation was to have over six hundred staff, making it one of the town's largest employers.

FINDING AN OFFICE

The next task was to find a permanent headquarters for the Corporation. Initially, it had been hoped to move into the late 18th century Howden House. Although when first built, the house was regarded as the very latest in domestic architecture, it was soon obvious that it was totally unsuited to the needs of a mid 20th century office. There was no option but to build a new headquarters for a new town. A site in Livingston Village was acquired from the Rosebery family, plans were drawn up and a contractor appointed.

In August, 1963, the Secretary of State for Scotland, Michael Noble started the machine which drove the first pile for the foundations of the Corporation's new headquarters. After some technical delays, the first staff moved in during 1965. As staff numbers increased, an extension had to be built and several departments rehoused in offices throughout the town. The Corporation moved into its second last headquarters, Sidlaw House, in the town centre in 1984.

While the office was being built, staff were housed in various temporary locations in Edinburgh, starting out life in rooms within the Scottish Office, then moving to The Scotsman building which was at least convenient for press relations, and finally to larger offices in Melville Street.

HOUSING THE STAFF

Staff not only needed office accommodation but also a home. Although Craigshill was the first area to be developed, it was decided to build the initial houses in the established community of Livingston Station. The enthusiasm to make a start was such that the Corporation's Secretary had to remind the Board of the wisdom of seeking competitive tenders, a reminder which was to prove timely. The contractor who submitted the lowest tender moved on site. Suddenly work was halted due to financial difficulties from which the contractor never recovered. Tam Dalyell, the recently elected MP for West Lothian, later asked a question in the House about the wisdom of appointing the contractor; demonstrating the sense of James Kelly's advice.

Change of Address
Located in the heart of Livingston Village, this was the third of the Corporation's five headquarters and the first to be purpose-built. Before Kirk Lane came North Bridge and Melville Street in Edinburgh: to come was Sidlaw House, Almondvale and Bell Square, Brucefield Industrial Park.

The First Three Chairmen
The first two Chairmen, Sir David Lowe and William Taylor were invited back to Livingston in 1974 by the third Chairman Dr Desmond Misselbrook along with other past Board members to see how far the town had progressed.

MEETINGS AND MORE MEETINGS

In the first year, the Board met on fourteen occasions, although it was soon to settle into a regular pattern with meetings, held on the third Friday of every month. Initially, a team of civil servants was in attendance to give guidance and ensure that the correct procedures were established. Although for the first few months, the Board reported to the Secretary of State for Scotland, through the Department of Health, it soon came under the wing of the newly formed Scottish Development Department which brought together economic development and physical planning.

As well as eight Board Committees looking at specific aspects of the town's development and weekly management meetings, the Corporation was also represented on the Joint Planning Advisory Committee and its five working groups, supervising the preparation of the Lothians Regional Survey and Plan.

Before building could start, there were a host of organisations to consult and joint policies to be worked out, from discussions with Glasgow Corporation on how overspill would work to sorting out with the two County Councils responsibilities for the provision of sewerage and water facilities and negotiating with local landowners including the characterful Dr Isaac Newton, owner of Murieston House.

1,001 THINGS TO DO

In building a new town, where do you start? The answer was to study the site from all angles. A detailed aerial survey was commissioned, while engineers test bored the first building sites. The first year was a period of immense and varied activity. An application was made to make the town a smokeless zone and the decision taken to establish a tree and plant nursery. The industrial development section were busy from the start negotiating with potential incoming firms and planning the first advanced factories. As well as designing the road network for the town, the engineers had to contend with the major issue of the proposed M8 where the views of the Corporation and the Scottish Office differed on the preferred alignment.

ITCHY FEET

The Board were naturally keen to learn from the experience of others. A Board trip to Scandinavia to study the architecture of new communities was vetoed by a Government Minister. The Board had to make do with a rather more mundane tour of Basildon, Bracknell, Hemel Hempstead and Stevenage new towns. Members also met in

Cumbernauld, which was already attracting headlines for its radical architecture and unusually compact design.

Another proposed foreign visit turned out to be extremely productive. Through his aerospace contacts, Board member, William Miller, learned that the US supplier to Rolls Royce was considering setting up a plant in Europe. Brigadier Purches was hastily dispatched across the Atlantic to clinch the deal with Cameron Iron Works.

COLD FEET

Occasionally, the Board showed some trepidation as to the enormity of the task before it. In the first annual report, the Chairman complained that the Secretary of State had not provided "as has normally been done, a draft Master Plan or the vast quantity of detailed and valuable research material necessary in its compilation" On the other hand, the Board was also nervous about the setting up of the Joint Planning Advisory Committee which would in fact provide them with much of this research, on the grounds of "potential duplication and conflict of ideas on how Livingston should develop." In practice, these fears proved groundless.

On other issues, the Board showed remarkable foresight. In that very first year, it voiced concern about the risks of being too dependent on a single industry, although suppliers to the new BMC factory at Bathgate were a natural target in the attraction of industry. Members also decided to set aside land for private housing to achieve their ultimate aim of a balanced community. The importance of the environment to the town's future was recognised in decisions as varied as developing a policy of re-using listed buildings to making the town a smokeless zone.

MOVING TOWARDS THE MASTER PLAN

Work started on the Master Plan, the definitive statement on how the town would develop, in early 1963. As work progressed, a number of advance decisions were taken. The preservation of Livingston Village was important to give the new town a sense of its past. Similarly, a Tree Preservation Order was applied for to protect the shelter belts and parkland which gave the raw landscape continuity until new plantings could take hold. An immediate start was made to Houstoun Industrial Estate as enquiries from industry were already coming in.

Creative Chaos

"The first thing we had to do in establishing an office was to find some furniture. Some was constructed from old cupboards which we found lying about. It has been in the Corporation's inventory ever since. The office was a sea of chaos, a veritable battleground between the planners and the engineers. You would find a dozen people with magic markers and plans all round the room looking at Craigshill and the industrial area to the north. One architect was sketching the "stoop and room" system used in the shale mines. Why she was doing this I don't know but it was inspirational. All in all, it was endlessly busy and endlessly frantic but it was really exciting and great fun".

Ken Anderson, Head Of Engineering

Master Minds
The slim volume of the Master Plan contrasts with the two volume, 1966 Lothians Regional Survey and Plan with its 32 chapters, 17 appendices and 250 tables. The latter was masterminded by Professor D J Robertson of Glasgow University and Sir Robert Matthew and Professor Percy Johnson-Marshall of Edinburgh University.

5
·THE MASTER PLAN·

Preparing the Master Plan for a new town amounted to no less than drawing a map of the future, defining how people may live, work and enjoy their leisure for many years to come. As the term Master Plan suggests, earlier new town planners tended to make the map fairly detailed, precise and fixed. By and large, this was not the style adopted by Peter Daniel and his team, to some extent from choice but also because the limited time available and the size and complexity of the task only permitted a fairly general approach. In retrospect this can be seen as the beginning of a more strategic approach to planning in which aims, assumptions and principles are set out clearly before the detail is filled in.

A NEW TOWN IN SIX MONTHS

In designating a new town the Government sometimes chose to appoint consultants to prepare the Master Plan during the process of designation. This was then adopted by the Corporation for implementation, often after introducing some judicious changes to make it more realistic. A different approach was taken for Livingston partly because the Corporation was expected to work closely with the very recently appointed consultants preparing the regional plan for what was to become the Greater Livingston Area. While this had the advantage that the Corporation would not have to accept a plan it was unhappy with, the drawback was that the planners had to start from scratch in undertaking the necessary survey work as well as preparing the plan in a very short time.

On arrival at the Development Corporation's temporary Edinburgh office in January 1963, Peter Daniel's first priority was to put together a team of architects, planners, engineers and landscape architects to work on the Plan. They were young and enthusiastic, keen to start on the challenge of a lifetime. In addition to Daniel himself, several brought with them experience of working in other new towns. One of the researchers who worked on the Lothians Regional Survey consultancy team was Dr Peter McGovern who joined the Corporation as Assistant Chief Planner early in 1963, thus helping the vital dialogue between the two organisations.

An intensive examination of the 6,692 acres of the designated area got underway. Its rural tranquillity was now regularly disturbed by surveyors with theodolites, bus tours of Board Members, officials familiarising themselves with their territory and arboriculturalists checking the condition of woodlands. Peter Daniel himself was found on one occasion perched in a tree sketching out his vision of some future aspect of the town.

Meanwhile in the turrets of The Scotsman building high above Princes Street the Corporation's office was a sea of creative chaos with maps, drawings and graphs covering every available space. One of the team recalls how blood was spilled when minutes before a critical presentation to the Board, an over enthusiastic wielder of a Stanley knife adorned a map with more red shading than had been intended.

In the process of preparing the Plan, a large number of options for the overall layout of the town were evaluated. This work had to be fitted in with the even more pressing task of determining the best location for the first housing developments. Liaison with the Regional Plan team was almost continuous, so closely were the two exercises linked. Meanwhile proposals for the alignment of the new M8 motorway were emerging and the Corporation had to engage in battle to resist the road being taken south of Dechmont Law, well into the designated area and threatening to cleave the town in two.

Peter Daniel's team was under immense pressure to deliver. While work on the Plan was still underway, the first housing projects were about to start on site at Livingston Station. The Scottish Office was constantly reminding the Corporation of the target of 1,000 houses a year laid down in the Draft Designation Order. After what must have seemed an eternity to those waiting, although in reality little more than six months, the draft Master Plan was presented to the Board in November, 1963. It was a remarkable achievement and a testimony to those involved.

The achievement, however, was not without its casualties. The group preparing the Master Plan had to work with a Board and senior management team who were still feeling their way and establishing their style of working. From the start there was friction between Peter Daniel, the creative architect and Brigadier Purches, whose military background gave him an ordered, 'no nonsense' approach to managing the development of the town.

Executive meetings were likened to tennis matches between these two strong personalities with the other members watching from the sidelines. Occasionally they would put forward a suggestion or comment on the design of a building only to have

Livingston from Space
This satellite view of Central Scotland was one of many produced by the Livingston company, ERSAC who specialised in processing satellite communications.

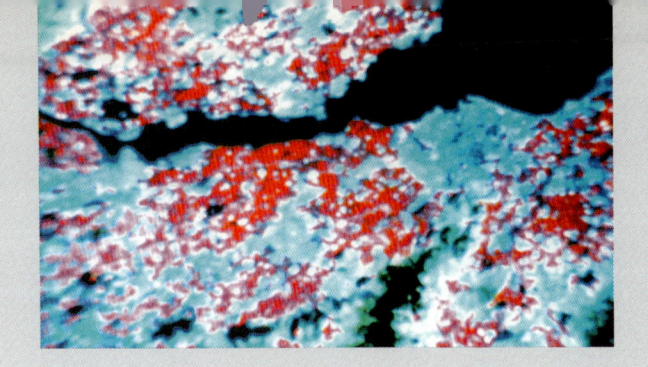

their views ruled out of court. Eventually matters came to a head and in November, 1964, Daniel resigned, to be followed by several members of his staff in the succeeding months. In the aftermath, the tension of a potentially very serious situation was defused by the pragmatic Construction Manager who reminded colleagues that their job was now "to get on and get Livingston built."

THE BLUEPRINT FOR LIVINGSTON

The 62 densely typed foolscap sheets, 18 maps and diagrams bound in a modest grey cover belie the importance of the Master Plan report. It was the blueprint for Livingston, setting out how the town would develop from three villages into the centre of a new region and determining the phasing of each stage in reaching the ultimate goal. This was done, in what was for its time, a remarkably disciplined and logical style.

The point of departure was a statement of the purpose of the town and the size of the target population as set out in the Draft Designation Order. From this were derived six fundamental principles for the development of Livingston which were carried through into almost every aspect of the Plan.

The Master Plan identified the outstanding quality of the natural environment within the designated area and the need to retain this within the future urban fabric of the town. In order to provide continuity with the past, it proposed that a purpose should be found for existing buildings of historical or architectural interest. In these and many other respects, Livingston today has the features of the town envisaged in 1963.

MAKING SPACE FOR PEOPLE

The Master Plan was designed on the basis of a target population of 70,000 immigrants with an additional 30,000 coming from "natural increase." The Lothians Regional Survey and Plan had argued for an even more ambitious target of 120,000 but this was rejected, wisely in the light of events. Given the need to accommodate 100,000 people, much energy was devoted to working out how to fit the required number of houses together with all the other necessary land uses into a very tight geographical area while allowing the variation in housing densities that would differentiate Livingston from the monotony of many 1950s Council housing estates.

After setting aside areas for the town centre, industrial estates, roads and open space, the land left for housing necessitated an average residential density of 59 people per acre. In order to encourage and cater for the diversity of housing characteristic of an established town, individual site densities were to range from 200 people an acre in the residential districts around the town centre to 30 per acre in the outer suburbs.

In the event, nothing approaching the higher densities was ever built. Livingston was fortunate in narrowly missing the era when buildings such as tower blocks and walk-up flats were seen as the chief solution to housing need and in many places implemented on a grand, even grandiose scale. The medium density developments in Craigshill proved sufficiently problematic and unpopular with tenants to ensure that an even more cautious and conservative approach was adopted thereafter.

A TOWN DESIGNED FOR THE CAR

The second major influence on the proposed form of the town was the private car given the widely held assumption that within a decade or two it would be universally affordable. More than simply a means of transport, the car was seen as a symbol of vitality and progress. "It is essential that the town should as soon as possible present both to the region and its own inhabitants a symbol of the age in which we live. It is proposed that the region/town road system will be such a symbol". The overall skeleton of the town and the shape of the districts within it were determined, therefore, by the system of town, regional and town-regional connector roads in the form of a rather complicated grid. They were to be tied into each other and to district distributor roads by means of grade separated junctions, thus dispensing with the need for traffic lights.

This preoccupation with the car, which reflected the conventional thinking of the time, resulted in public transport almost being relegated to a footnote in the report. "Ways of providing bus services will be discussed with the bus companies and the road authorities". Not surprisingly, it soon became evident that this was one of the main shortcomings of the plan and one which would not be easily remedied.

Wherever possible, in residential areas pedestrians and vehicles were to be strictly segregated. The Master Plan adopted the Radburn system, originally conceived for a garden suburb of that name in New Jersey in 1928. The aim was to provide residents with access to local shops and schools without having to cross a road. This was achieved by building houses in cul de sacs and similar groupings with one side of each of each house facing onto a separate footpath. These paths then joined a town wide network taking people across main roads by foot bridges or underpasses. This theory, embodied in the Master Plan's approach, was widely applied in the design of the town's districts.

A Town of Principle
Six fundamental principles guided the Master Plan.
- *The design of the town must have a distinctive structure and character related to the physical environment and its local and regional purpose.*
- *Good landscape must be conserved and created.*
- *The highest standards of industrial and residential layout and design must be achieved.*
- *A positive effort will be made to achieve a balance of population in relation to age groups, family structure and employment*
- *Complete self-containment is not visualised.*
- *The motor vehicle must be so controlled as to allow a maximum degree of pedestrian insulation.*

The Map of the Future
By moving two industrial areas outside the designated area, the 1966 Master Plan revision allowed the housing densities adopted in the 1963 Plan to be dramatically reduced.

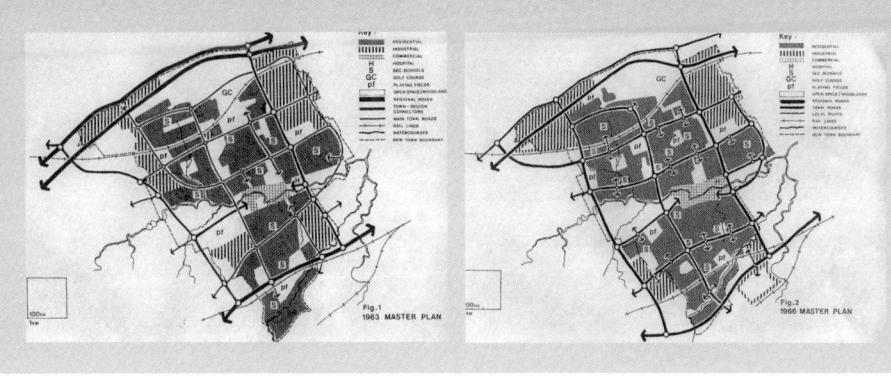

DISTRICTS AND CENTRE

The grid of the road system was to divide the town into "environmental districts" insulated from the effects of through traffic. Ten of the districts were zoned predominantly for housing and four for industry while the town centre was to sit strategically astride the river, linking the areas to the north and the south. The Plan departed from the approach of earlier new towns of creating neighbourhoods, each with its own school, shops, Church and amenities. In Livingston, a more flexible approach was adopted which recognised the need for adjacent districts to share facilities in situations where a different size of population catchment was required than the district alone could provide. Although a logical and resource efficient approach, this caused some misunderstanding with residents who naturally wished their district to be as well provided for as they felt the one next door to be.

Even with this approach the implications of building 1,000 houses per annum were daunting. A church, community hall or health centre would be required every six months, a primary school every year and a secondary school every two and a half years. A sports pitch or play area would have to be created every month for the next twenty years.

In the Master Plan, a great deal of emphasis was placed on the form and function of the town centre. It was intended that the elements of the centre would be built as a series of structures within the setting of the central valley, integrated with lakes and landscape features. At the eastern end would be an elegant bridge carrying the main spine road across the Almond and in the west where the valley opened out, a special reservation was set aside, destined one day to become Kirkton Campus. The Central Valley was to be the main focus of a network of open spaces which would conserve the area's attractive natural features.

There is repeated emphasis in the Plan on the importance of the town's role as a centre for the whole region, the Greater Livingston Growth Area. It is made clear that the town centre and the standard of the road system would have to be of the highest quality if this inspiration was to be realised.

A BALANCED COMMUNITY

A theme running through the Master Plan was the need to create a diverse and balanced community. The experience of other new towns had shown the importance of attracting a wide range of age and income groups. Achieving this would depend on a number of factors in particular diversity of employment opportunities and a good variety of housing. The right mix of community and cultural facilities would need to be secured at each stage of the town's development, bearing in mind the changing makeup of the population as the town matured. If Livingston failed to retain its young people who had grown up in the town "kinship groups will be broken with possible ill health and unhappiness and the town will lack the social, cultural and economic diversity of established places".

ACHIEVING THE VISION

Much of the Plan was devoted to how it was to be implemented. Not surprisingly in view of the work of the architects proceeding in parallel with the Master Plan process, there was much comment on the logistics of industrialised house building. The intended pattern of phasing of development and the corresponding build up of population was also described in some detail. Apart from one early housing project and the industrial estate at Deans, development was to proceed from east to west in strips, each of which would work outwards from the centre to the north and south. While inevitably there have been departures from this arrangement, by and large it has been followed as a broad strategy through to the present time with Adambrae and Eliburn Campus remaining on the west side of the town as the only major undeveloped areas.

In 1964 the Master Plan was approved by the Board with very few changes and submitted to the Secretary of State by the end of the year. The Board's amendments included deleting the reference to the need for a family planning clinic and a dog pound in the town. In practice, before long there was a need for both.

A CONTINUING PROCESS

The Master Plan report made it clear that its outline proposals would not only require adjustment to tie in with the recommendations of the Lothian Regional Survey and Plan, but would need to be to be kept under more or less continuous review. By the time the Regional Survey and Plan was published in 1966 much more research on the proposals had been carried out and in September of that year a short review of the Master Plan was submitted to the Board. This adopted the regional planners' suggestion that two industrial areas should be relocated outside the designated area thus enabling a dramatic reduction in the proposed housing densities. The nettle of public transport began to be grasped. A bus service would run throughout the

"It should be possible for every family to live in a clean, healthy and reasonably spacious home equipped with the latest labour-saving devices, carefully planned in a well designed neighbourhood and community, with the surrounding open space landscaped by the best team of landscape architects available."
Lothians Regional Survey and Plan, 1966

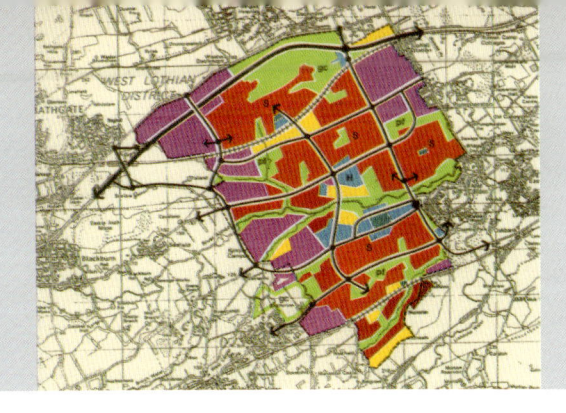

The Master Plan Revisited
Later revisions of the Master Plan in 1979 and a decade later reflect the final shape of the town.

districts on the local distributor roads, bringing services within a quarter of a mile of every home. This obliged routes to be circuitous proving a source of much frustration to passengers and drivers alike.

By this time progress was well underway with the preparation, in line with statutory requirements, of detailed district 'Stage A' plans which started with Craigshill in 1965 and ended in 1995 with Adambrae. Each of these plans extended and interpreted the outlines of the Master Plan. A consolidation of the Master Plan was undertaken in 1972 for the town's 10th anniversary celebrations accompanied by a major public exhibition staged in the newly opened Howden Park Centre.

As the newly constituted Lothian Regional Council began to stretch its wings in 1976 it started to challenge certain principles and assumptions of the Master Plan. The Corporation was uncertain whether the best response was to continue with its intended review of the Plan, thus exposing itself to public debate, or to batten down the hatches and wait until the storm had passed. It decided on the former course of action embarking on an extended period of policy review which ended three years later with the publication of the Livingston Plan 1979.

This was a comprehensive corporate statement, the subject of extensive public and technical consultation. It successfully consolidated the Corporation's position in relation to the Regional Council who now pronounced Livingston "the jewel in its crown" as a result of the town's outstanding economic performance.

A final review of the Plan was undertaken in 1989 following on from the preparation of the Corporation's review of its 1983 Development Profile. This had been requested by the Scottish Office to demonstrate how much was left to be done before the Corporation was ready to be wound up. In all of these reviews, one trend was consistent; a reduction in the population capacity of the designated area. For many years, the target of 70,000 or 100,000 had been a virility symbol for the Corporation, not to be challenged despite the growing evidence. By the early 1990s, however, it was clear that the town's capacity was less than 60,000 and the Corporation was by now mature enough to acknowledge it publicly.

In announcing the Corporation's wind-up date as 1996, the Secretary of State stipulated that before then, West Lothian District Council would need to have an adopted local plan in place. In fact, the Council had already taken the imaginative step of commissioning the Corporation's Planning Department to prepare such a plan on its behalf, making Livingston probably the only British new town to be invited to carry out this task. Following a Public Inquiry into the plan in 1995, it was finally adopted by the Council in March, 1996 returning Livingston to a normal local authority planning regime after 34 years, with the rescinding of its Special Development Order.

Over the decades this Order had empowered the Corporation to act as a delegated planning authority, a crucial ingredient in the one-door approach which proved so effective in attracting development. When they decided to move in, inward investors naturally wanted instant decisions, Those Development Corporations like Livingston which had planning powers were in the enviable position of being able to provide sites, finance and planning permission as part of an integrated package. In its last two years, the Corporation authorised building developments of over £400m, a significant proportion of which came from businesses keen to establish or expand in the town.

The Curious Garden
Remaining true to the Master Plan's principle of conserving the environment, in Peel Park, the Corporation marked out the site of the 17th century "curious garden" of over 1,000 species which was created by Sir Patrick Murray in the grounds of Livingston Peel. On his death, the eminent physician, Sir Robert Sibbald transferred the plants to his new physic garden, which formed the nucleus of Edinburgh's Royal Botanic Garden. Some of the trees in Peel Park may have been planted by Sir Patrick's nephew who shared his love of gardening.

·PEOPLE WORK AND PLACE·

6
·A PLACE FOR PEOPLE·

In selecting the site for Scotland's fourth new town, one of the criteria stipulated by the civil servants was the location's ability to support a population of up to 70,000. The Order designating Livingston as the Government's final choice gave as one of its justifications "that the area could accommodate an interesting and compact town of 70,000 persons in conditions of high amenity." In April, 1962, Livingston had a population of just over 2,000. Three hundred people lived in the farms and farmworkers' cottages scattered throughout the designated area while the remainder were residents of the three villages.

Forecasting the town's population growth was critical, as planning the provision of schools, shops and amenities depended on getting the figures right. Planning was further complicated by the fact that Livingston did not fit within any existing boundaries for data collection, from the Census to unemployment statistics. Initial estimates were made on the assumption that it would be possible to build 1,000 houses a year between 1965 and 1984. In planning the New Town, therefore, a target population of 100,000 was adopted, 70% of which would be achieved by attracting new residents from outside the area and the rest by natural growth. Thus by 1985, Livingston would need to attract 56,000 incoming residents to reach its immediate target population of 70,000. The ultimate target of 100,000 would be reached by the early years of the next Millennium.

It was envisaged that the new residents would come from a variety of sources including employees of the nearby BMC tractor plant, residents of the traditional coal mining villages of Midlothian and West Lothian and even emigrants from Edinburgh. 80% of the new residents, however, were to be recruited from Glasgow as part of what was known as the overspill programme.

OVERSPILL

Why did Glaswegians opt for a new life in the unfamiliar territory of a new town and even more so in Livingston which could be seen as within the enemy camp of Edinburgh. "We wanted the kids to have a new start in life." "I grew up in a tenement close to the Bar-L and I didn't want to spend the rest of my life overlooking a prison." "I got a job with Cameron's - it was too good an opportunity to miss." "I visited my sister who had already taken the plunge. Her house was so neat and new that I had to have the same."

Overspill involved encouraging people from Glasgow and later West Central Scotland to move to the new towns or other expanding centres in Scotland. In the 1950s and 60s, Glasgow Corporation established arrangements with the four new towns and 60 local authorities from Wick to Haddington to take its excess population. Although in practice, the agreement with many local authorities remained largely on paper with residents resistant to the idea of their community being swamped by city dwellers, some West Lothian towns including Polbeth, Blackburn and Whitburn actively participated in overspill. Their co-operation may have helped in the decision to site Livingston close by.

The Corporation's original letting policy very much

Did He Stay?
One early resident accosted a local minister in desperation. Where was the betting shop? There was none. Where was the nearest pub? East Calder. In that case, where was the bus? There was none.

Rev Hamish Smith, Ecumenical team minister

The 7,000th House

The Corporation's 7,000th house was let to a young family from Cornwall in March, 1976. Its 5,000th, 33 Willowbank, Ladywell was a three apartment terraced house with a fitted kitchen and coloured bathroom suite complete with shower. Opened by the Lord Provost of Glasgow, it was a showhouse during the 10th birthday celebrations.

reflected the categories of resident which it wished to attract. Top of the list were Glasgow's overspill nominees and others with a job in one of the town's industries and employees of firms in the surrounding area notably BMC, followed by relatives of residents and over time second generation families. Smaller categories included construction workers and local authority employees.

The initial vetting of residents was strict. Families were adopted by Glasgow Corporation which agreed to contribute £14 annually over a ten year period for each house rented to a nominated family. There had to be a firm prospect of a job in the new town. In order to reduce the city's jobless, the Government offered unemployed people willing to look for work in Livingston, assistance with fares and lodging as well as a £400 cash bonus when they moved.

After the initial drive which came close to achieving its initial target of 1,000 Glasgow overspill tenants, by the late 1960s, the impetus slackened. Livingston drew more and more of its residents from the East of Scotland and the Borders. Some people came from much further afield. A small but enthusiastic group from Wales ensured that rugby soon became a sporting fixture in the town, setting up reciprocal arrangements with a Welsh supporters club in Cilfynedd.

RENEWED EFFORTS

With Special Development Area status being granted in 1971 only on condition that Livingston took 60% of its residents from West Central Scotland in the first year and 80% a year thereafter, recruitment efforts doubled. Livingston and Glenrothes, which was faced with the same demand, jointly set up a caravan in central Glasgow under the "Better Living" banner and toured housing estates looking for tenants. A major advertising campaign was launched in the "Daily Record" and the "Evening Times". A free weekend bus service ran from Glasgow to Livingston to allow prospective tenants to see the town for themselves.

The result was that the town's population virtually doubled in the next five years, increasing from 16,500 to 30,000. By 1974, Livingston was the largest town in the whole of the Lothians outside Edinburgh. This, however, was achieved by taking non priority applications from the waiting list and the original vetting criteria were virtually abandoned. Families moved into Livingston without a job, at a time when the town's unemployment was on the increase. Most of the new residents were given houses in Craigshill, Ladywell and Knightsridge, placing enormous pressure on schools and community resources. Employment could not keep up with this very rapid expansion, with some residents experiencing the hardships of poverty and unemployment.

By no means everyone who came to Livingston

stayed. In the 1970s, the annual turnover of residents regularly exceeded 10%. People left because of the higher cost of living, unemployment or simple homesickness, unable to settle away from the ties of home and family.

GOING AFTER THE GRANNIES

In the early years, like most of its counterparts, Livingston was "a ghost town" at weekends when many residents went back to their old homes to visit parents and friends. Recognising the importance of bringing older people into the new town to achieve a more balanced community and to help young families to settle, Corporation staff actively promoted the benefits of the new town for older people. In 1971, they brought out the first edition of "Enjoy Your Retirement in Livingston". As the resident population grew older, however and transport services improved, it was no longer necessary to import the grannies. For many years, elderly relatives of existing residents remained a priority category when letting houses.

WHERE DID THEY COME FROM?

As Livingston's second generation grew up, the gap between new comers and established townspeople narrowed. By 1979, more than half of the incoming population came from within the Lothians, a trend that was to increase still further as Livingston became more attractive to private housing developers.

In parallel, the intake from West Central Scotland fell significantly. While the population of Glasgow dropped dramatically, communities like Bishopbriggs and Erskine on its periphery expanded. The rehabilitated tenements and increasingly the building of new low cost private housing on gap sites within the city itself provided new opportunities for the young families on whom most new towns had traditionally relied for their incoming populations.

Although Livingston has drawn most of its population from within Scotland's Central Belt, it has always welcomed people from further afield. In 1972, the Corporation agreed to house Ugandan Asians, expelled from their adopted country during the regime of Idi Amin. The first family to choose Livingston from the Resettlement Board contained two electrical engineers. Later, the Corporation was to make the same welcoming gesture to the Vietnamese boat people. Today, around one in ten of the town's population comes from South of the Border and 3%, from further afield.

CENSUSES AND SURVEYS

Livingston's population was first put under official scrutiny in the 1971 Census although the full results would not be published for several years. By then,

---

First Impressions

"The town should have been built awa' up on the Lang Whang."

"It is very interesting being in a space age town."

"The mud was like the trenches in the First World War."

"It was a Klondyke town."

"Some of the kids had never seen cows before."

"When I saw how good and clean it was, I resolved to get a job and a house."

Taking the Corporation to Town
Flares may be coming back into fashion but a flair for publicity was always a key Corporation attributes. Its mobile caravan, here manned by Desmond McGimpsey the Corporation's PRO in Ladywell, helped keep local residents informed of new developments..

the town's population had risen to 14,000, albeit well short of the expansion envisaged in the Master Plan. Given that population, housing and jobs were all part of the same complex equation, this was not surprising, with a slow start to the housing programme being followed by the recession of 1970.

At a national level, the 1971 Census sounded the early warning signals that the years of spectacular population growth were over, with the population of most Scottish towns and cities, at best remaining static. Livingston's natural growth targets, however, still looked promising. In 1971, the town's birth rate was double the national average with 84% of the population aged under 40.

The next year, one wit put forward the explanation for this when he wrote at the foot of his survey form that "the lack of entertainment for adults has resulted in a comparatively high birth rate." This Household Survey was the Development Corporation's first formal exercise in gathering its own data about the town and in consulting its residents, The results were used by staff for a range of purposes, from population projections to house design,

The Development Corporation, however, was not the first organisation to canvass the views of residents. That distinction belonged to the pupils of Craigshill High who in 1970 asked local primary pupils what they liked and disliked about the town. They liked the underpasses and the types of housing but were critical of shopping, buses and jobs. The three amenities which they would most like to see were a swimming pool, an ice rink and a cinema.

The dislikes of the town's adult residents as quantified by the 1972 Household Survey mirrored those of the younger generation. Satisfaction with the Corporation's housing was high, except for the black paintwork of some Craigshill houses and interest in home ownership was also strong. Two thirds of residents had chosen to come to the town for its positive qualities rather than from the desire simply to move away from the "unattractiveness of their previous residence." Around a fifth, however, were considering leaving the town in the next two years, because of lack of employment opportunities, high prices or in the hope of being in a position to buy a house.

The Development Corporation repeated the exercise in 1977, seeking this time to obtain more detail on tenants' views of their houses as well as to find out about the increasing number of residents who were not Corporation tenants. Although overall findings were relatively comparable, the survey showed how much the town had moved on in the short space of five years. Encouragingly, two thirds of those who had left existing households had set up a new home in the town. With the Livingston Centre recently opened, already nearly three quarters of residents were doing their weekly shop in Almondvale. Concerns centred more on the lack of entertainment especially for young people and the perennial issue of the bus services which was becoming more acute as the town grew larger.

In 1983, the Livingston Voluntary Organisations Council took up the mantle from the Corporation of testing residents' opinions, enlisting the support of a team of Moray House students to carry out the field work. They discovered that residents liked many aspects of their town - the schools, libraries, town centre shopping and facilities for older people. Their concerns centred on employment opportunities for young people, the lack of nurseries and the familiar themes of the bus services and lack of entertainment.

A MATURING COMMUNITY

In 1981, Livingston made national headlines as Britain's youngest town. In the 1980s, overall growth slowed down, with only an 11% increase in population between the 1981 and 1991 Censuses compared with 63% the previous decade. The 1991 Census confirmed that the population was also growing older. Although still a young town, children now accounted for a quarter rather than a third of the population and the proportion of those over state retirement age although still small was growing. Along with the trend for smaller families, the older population meant that the size of households was also becoming smaller, changing from close to 3.5 persons per household in 1971 to 2.8 twenty years later.

As yet, with a population of just over 45,000, Livingston has not even reached the half way point to the target of 100,000 people envisaged in the Master Plan, much less the goal of 120,000 proposed in the Lothians Regional Survey and Plan. There are two main reasons for this. Nationally, the post-War baby boom not only stopped but was reversed to the point when in the late 1980s, concerns focused on the impact of an increasingly elderly population and a reduced proportion of young people, the age group on which new towns traditionally drew for their incoming residents. The other was a complete shift in thinking about the role of cities in the early 1970s, moving away from the need for emigration to encouraging people back into the inner cities as a means of promoting urban regeneration.

For Livingston, the changing demographics were to be a blessing in disguise. Today's different industrial requirements and housing densities mean that there simply would not have been the capacity within the designated area to house a population of 70,000 much less 100,000 or 120,000.

__Lonely Hearts Club__
Despite events like Galas, people could be lonely in a strange town. One of the Corporation's many efforts to tackle the so-called New Town Blues came in 1973 with its Bureau for Lonely People. Candidates, nominated by doctors, ministers and health visitors were profiled and matched by Community Development staff who then put lonely residents in touch with each other.

First Day Cover
With one brief exception, the Corporation remained true to its simple but effective advertising slogan "Make it in Livingston" for over twenty years. Livingston was the first Scottish new town to advertise in the London underground. Even more imaginative marketing solutions were sometimes adopted. The Corporation took advantage of the first day cover for Information Technology Year in 1982 to mail thousands of brochures to electronics and health care companies in the United States, and the next year, repeated the exercise using the stamp commemorating the centenary of David Livingstone.

7
MAKING IT IN LIVINGSTON

"Make it in Livingston" was the message used by the Development Corporation for over twenty years to sell the benefits of the town to industry. A German businessman might see the phrase when he opened his daily newspaper or a manager in a Japanese electronics company on opening the mail. Millions of commuters must have caught a glimpse of Livingston as they travelled up the escalators of the London Underground.

These words were no empty slogan. One of Livingston Development Corporation's essential purposes and acknowledged achievements has been its ability to attract businesses to the town and to provide the environment for them to grow.

A TWO COMPANY TOWN
In 1962, there were only two companies employing just over two hundred people within the designated area of Livingston; the centuries old paper mill of Adam Robertson and Co Ltd, which now produces board for cartons using recycled materials, and Roneo Ltd, suppliers of office duplicators. After a relatively slow start, employment doubled in the early 1970s and doubled again during the 1980s. Today, over 30,000 people work in over 900 businesses and public services based in the town. What lies behind this considerable achievement? What were the milestones and setbacks on the way?

A FOCAL POINT FOR GROWTH
From the start, Livingston's primary purpose was economic. Two of the three tasks assigned to the new Development Corporation by the Secretary of State for Scotland were to strengthen the Scottish economy by providing a place where industry could flourish and to create a focal point for the growth of the regional economy, west of Edinburgh. When the third task of accommodating Glasgow's overspill population was finally abandoned in the mid-1970s, Livingston's role was focused even more on becoming a centre of local and national growth.

The importance of these tasks was recognised by the Board of the Development Corporation from the outset. It sought to address all aspects of economic development including advance factory building, marketing and the provision of training resources to match the skills of local people to the needs of potential employers. One of the Board's first actions was to set up an Industrial Committee to work out how these tasks might be achieved and to start the long and often complex process of persuading businesses to have faith in the future of what at the time was largely green fields.

PLANNING FOR GROWTH

In drawing up the Master Plan, land for industry was a major concern. With increasing automation in manufacturing processes, there was some uncertainty as to how many people would need to be accommodated per acre. In order to provide room for companies to expand without having to move premises, it was envisaged that at least 1,000 acres of land would be required.

The planners set down how they saw the town's economy growing. They estimated that 45% of the town's residents would need employment and that around half of these jobs would be in the service sector. They did not treat Livingston as a self-contained economy but made allowance for commuting both into and out of the town. Anticipating the importance of scientific activity in the era of Harold Wilson's "white heat of technology", they set aside land in Kirkton "for a major development such as a large research institute, a major technical or teaching College or a University."

While most office accommodation would be built in the town centre, industry would largely be confined to the four, outer corners. This would provide residents with a short journey from home to workplace while keeping heavy traffic out of the centre. Industrial estates would be created with immediate access to the town's main roads and rapidly thereafter to the national transport network. If required, railway sidings could be built. Within residential areas, there would be some provision for small businesses, especially in the service sector.

THE FIRST INCOMERS

As with several aspects of the town's development, the start to attracting businesses was inauspicious, despite the Corporation's best endeavours. The first company to be signed up, S & M Fire Appliances of Edinburgh, never actually made the move. Fortunately, this disappointment was swiftly followed by three more positive events.

In 1963, Cameron Iron Works, the US engineering company founded by two Scots, announced plans to establish a plant on Houstoun Industrial Estate to make heavy forgings, chiefly for the aerospace industry. A factor in the decision was the offer of loan finance by the Development Corporation.

How Do You Spell Houstoun?
The estate on which Cameron Iron Works chose to locate was called after the nearby Houstoun Wood, although early Corporation documents spelt it as in the oil capital of Texas. By coincidence, Cameron Iron Works' headquarters were in Houston, Texas but the Corporation turned down its request to change the spelling of the industrial estate.

Made in Livingston

Shortbread, semiconductor wafers and sutures were only three of the products made in Livingston over the last 34 years. Others include discs for the fan blades of Boeing jets: gold foil for the titles of bestsellers:. Royal Warrant waterproof roofing material for Balmoral castle: Scotland's first hermetically sealed double glazing units: the first "Gene machines" to be manufactured in Europe: exotic breads for Marks & Spencer: Russell Athletic strips for the home team supporters: the first single wear contact lenses developed outside the US: beer cans for the UK's leading brands.

Once in full production, Cameron went on to employ close on a thousand people, in a factory housing Europe's largest and most advanced foundry press. The project architect assigned to the design of the Livingston plant by Cameron's consultants was William Newman Brown, who joined the Development Corporation shortly afterwards as its second Chief Architect and Planning Officer.

The quality of the plant's architecture and layout was recognised when it came second in a competition run by the Financial Times in 1969 to find Britain's best factory. Although it has since undergone several changes of ownership and market direction, as Wyman-Gordon the half a million sq ft factory is still a major employer in the town. The original 30,000 tonne press, which can inflict a weight equivalent to the Forth Bridge on steel, is still at the heart of the company's operations.

In 1964, John Laing set up a factory to produce concrete house panels for the Jespersen industrial building system which the Development Corporation had chosen for the first 1,000 houses at Craigshill. Establishing the means of building the town within its centre was a significant coup for the Corporation. Once the factory was operational, however, production difficulties emerged causing delays to the house building programme. The factory closed shortly after the problems with the Jespersen flats emerged in 1968.

The other incomer of 1964 remained in the town for many years. Yale and Towne took over a temporary factory in Deans to start manufacturing locks and other security fittings until the Development Corporation could build a permanent facility for the company on the estate. The plant, designed jointly by the company and the Development Corporation was the first rented factory in the UK to win a Pacemaker Award, given to the UK's ten best designed factories. Its Manager was also influential in setting up the Livingston Industrial and Commercial Association, which for many years acted as the business voice of the town.

RECESSION AND ROLLS ROYCE

Despite these successes, business was slow to gather momentum and employment fell short of the target of 1,000 new jobs a year laid down in the Master Plan. By the end of the decade, just over twenty companies had set up in the town. When recession hit the UK in 1970 after many years of steady growth, it came as a particular shock in Livingston. Many residents had bought the package of a new job and a new house in a new town, as a means of moving away from the uncertainty of work in the shipyards and mines.

Cameron Iron Works had already made some workers redundant due to delays in the programme to build Concorde. In the run up to the crash of the aerospace company, Rolls Royce, for whom Cameron produced forgings for the RB111 engine, the company was forced to lay off hundreds of workers at short notice in the run up to Christmas. The town was devastated but not defeated. Neighbours rallied round to make up Christmas parcels for families whose breadwinner had been made redundant and the Churches offered their support. In those dark days, Livingston's community spirit was put to the test and not found wanting.

To make matters worse, enquiries from companies thinking of setting up in the town had been reduced to a trickle by the recession. The Board resolved to step up the effort to attract new business and to put Livingston on the international map. The industrial development and PR budgets were doubled. Spreading the message, however, started at home. As part of the town's 10th anniversary celebrations in 1972, the Corporation staged a major industrial exhibition in a show house factory on Houstoun Industrial Estate. Over forty of the town's businesses took a stand to display their products and capabilities at LINDEX. Industrialists throughout Central Scotland and further afield were invited to see for themselves the benefits that the new town could offer.

A SPECIAL DEVELOPMENT AREA

It took forward thinking, a degree of courage and a lot of imagination for some of the first companies to come to Livingston, at a time when the town was made up largely of fields with pockets of housing and construction sites. One of the main attractions in the era of acute labour shortages in the 1960s was Livingston's ability to draw not only on the local skills base but on potential employees who would move from areas of high unemployment, given the offer of a house. There was the added incentive of grants.

New towns were intended to encourage industry as well as people to move away from the congestion of cities, and to re-equip in modern factories. Glasgow Corporation offered assistance to companies wanting to move by helping them to dispose of their property and by adding their workers to the housing transfer list. Paterson's Shortbread was one of the very few companies to move from Glasgow to Livingston, partly as the result of taking over a bakery already in the town. Paterson's Burgh Bakery on Houstoun

Cooking with Gas
Proximity to the M8 was an important factor in attracting distribution companies to Livingston. One of the first was Scottish Gas who set up the UK's most advanced bulk storage handling facility of its day to serve domestic appliance retailers throughout Scotland. More recent arrivals include Booker McConnell, Dunkin Donuts, Hays, LIDL, Christian Salvesen and Tesco.

Industrial Estate which now manufactures oatcakes and biscuits as well as shortbread for world markets recalls the company's origins as a bakers in the former burgh of Rutherglen on the outskirts of the city.

In the 1960s, Government policy was very closely tied to unemployment. Through the Local Employment Act 1963, companies based in areas of high unemployment, designated Development Areas, were eligible for financial assistance if they created new jobs. Located in one of Scotland's growth areas, Livingston fell within this category

In 1971, the Government announced major changes to its regional policy. Companies located in areas experiencing economic decline were to be eligible not only for grants for additional workers but for new buildings and investment in machinery. The whole of the West of Scotland including its three new towns was declared a Special Development Area but Livingston and Glenrothes were excluded from the deal.

Both towns reacted quickly and decisively to the news, arguing that their fundamental purpose as economic growth centres would be lost if they could not offer incoming companies the best financial package. While the Board, Councillors and local MPs protested at the decision through formal channels, the people of Livingston added their weight to the campaign with the setting up of an action group against unemployment.

The campaign was successful. The Government awarded both towns Special Development Area status but on one condition, that they renewed their efforts to attract residents from areas of high unemployment in West Central Scotland. Although this decision would have significant repercussions on other aspects of the new town's development, it provided the incentive for business to make it in Livingston. Over the next decade, the number of businesses increased five fold.

Although there were further reviews of Government regional policy and changes in the types of grant, Livingston retained its ability to offer companies the maximum financial deal available outside the specially designated Enterprise Zones. It also shared in the assistance offered by the European Community to West Lothian as an area affected by the decline of heavy industry. The area's economic difficulties had been compounded when in 1983 British Leyland closed its Bathgate factory only three years after announcing plans to double its workforce, and the large Plessey capacitor plant shut down.

The Bathgate closure highlighted the role of Livingston within the wider regional economy. Although many Livingston residents lost their jobs when British Leyland and Plessey closed, unemployment within the town was falling at a time when the Bathgate area was one of Scotland's employment blackspots. The Development Corporation joined with other local and national agencies under the auspices of the Secretary of State's Working Party chaired by Gavin McCrone, to develop an action plan for the West Lothian economy. This resulted in the creation of Bathgate Area Support for Enterprise (BASE) and its successor, West Lothian Enterprise, to regenerate the area primarily through small business support and training. BASE extended its activities into the new town. Technically because of its location within a wider area of economic decline, Livingston remained eligible for European Regional Development Fund support despite its growth performance. The benefits of European and Development Area assistance continued through to the Corporation's final years

COMINGS AND GOINGS

In 1972 with the end of the recession and the securing of Special Development Area status, business picked up sharply, not only for Cameron Ironworks but for Livingston as a whole. The flow of new announcements gathered momentum. Several of the businesses which first set up in Livingston in the early to mid 1970s are still manufacturing in the town today, including Tulloch Engineering, EPS (Moulders) and Wilson Byard. Brooklyns Westbrick took over the former Laing factory to produce concrete goods for civil engineering. Pringle Knitwear promised hundreds of jobs although their actual stay was less than two years. Manufacturing cartons for the whisky industry, Ashton Containers provided a welcome source of employment for male workers, helping to meet some concerns that most of the new jobs at the time were for women.

The Brussels based, Red House (Rooflights) Ltd became the first company from the European Community to make it in Livingston. As for several other businesses, the town's own building programme provided an immediate market as well as a base from which to serve the rest of the UK. The first warehousing and distribution companies showed interest in the town's strategic position, a growing trend which was to contribute to the broadening of employment in the next two decades.

As in any industrial town, there were inevitably some casualties. Surprisingly Lee Cooper Jeans announced the doubling of its workforce in the middle of a four week strike which shortly afterwards was quoted as a contributory factor in the company's decision to pull out of the town. Some smaller companies from the South of England retreated after a few years on the grounds that Scotland had turned out to be too distant from their markets. The companies which stayed outweighed those which left and by the mid 1970s, those which stayed were expanding rapidly.

Making the Move
In 1975, the staff of George Whiley Ltd were shown round the town to assist in the company's decision to relocate from Croydon. The Corporation's 1981 annual report reiterated the role of the town in inward investment. "We are not just selling factory space: we are selling a town and that is what firms are looking for - good housing, good schools, a congenial atmosphere to live in."

***Healthy Business**
Surgikos (Arbrook) was one of first health care companies to decide to make it in Livingston, attracted by its manufacturing reputation and modern environment as well as proximity to Edinburgh's clinical excellence. Medical imaging, including several spin-offs from Nuclear Enterprises, pharmaceuticals and biotechnology are particular Livingston strengths.*

ESTATES FOR INDUSTRY

Holding a stock of modern industrial accommodation was a key weapon in Livingston's armoury in winning business. As set out in the Master Plan, Houstoun and Deans Industrial Estates, at the north east and north west corners of the town, were the first to be developed. Houstoun was adjacent to the M8 while Deans rapidly grew to the point where it straddled the motorway. Businesses could build their own facility by buying a site or by leasing it from the Development Corporation.

The Corporation also had the powers to build factories in anticipation of need, so that incoming firms could be accommodated quickly. A company could establish an office, or start up operations in a small factory immediately and then move to larger accommodation as soon as market demand justified increased production. The interiors of the Corporation's advance factories were designed to allow expansion of production or administration with the minimum of disruption. This flexibility extended to the way in which industrial estates were planned, permitting three or four smaller units to be combined to create a larger factory if required.

The Corporation also fitted out factories to meet the needs of individual tenants. In most cases, this was a relatively simple exercise, involving the creation of a new loading bay or rearranging the internal layout. As the town's success in attracting high technology companies grew, however, the Corporation's architects and engineers became expert in the complexities of clean rooms and uninterruptable power supplies

As soon as existing accommodation started to fill up, the Corporation would apply to the Scottish Office for authorisation to service more land or to build more factories. At times, given the stop-go performance of the UK economy, accurately forecasting the scale and nature of demand and maintaining a stock of factories of different sizes, ready to move into, was a feat of juggling for the Corporation's Estates and Marketing Department. This was further complicated by the need to reserve accommodation for any business which expressed serious interest in coming to Livingston, until such time as it made a final decision.

Room for expansion was often built in from the outset, in order not only to ensure that companies could grow but to avoid the unsightly back yards, typical of older factories. From the start, what distinguished Livingston's industrial estates from those in traditional manufacturing areas was the importance placed on creating an environment, appropriate to modern industries and their employees.

The nature of the manufacturing activities attracted to Livingston in the decade following the Master Plan, became quieter, cleaner, more automated and, therefore, more demanding of space, than the planners had anticipated. The design of advance factories and of industrial estates had to keep pace with this change in the operating environment. Looking to the future, Development Corporation staff visited the United States to study some of its industrial parks in order to replicate in Livingston a similar environment to that of the head offices of some of the businesses like W L Gore or Surgikos which they hoped to attract.

KIRKTON CAMPUS

In setting aside an area of Kirkton for research, the 1963 Master Plan not only showed remarkable foresight as to what the industries of the late 20th century would be but also provided those within the Corporation responsible for developing and marketing the site with a unique claim. Kirkton Campus was to become Scotland's first high technology park, designed exclusively for research and development orientated science businesses.

Kirkton Campus was a far-sighted and long term project, although not quite as ambitious as the very first plans for the site. One of the Development Corporation's first opportunities lay in persuading the proposed Heriot-Watt University to come to Livingston. This option, however, was rejected by the University in favour of the Riccarton Estate on the Western outskirts of Edinburgh. The deal was clinched by the astute offer by Midlothian County Council to transfer ownership of the land without cost to the University. In the view of its first Chief Architect and Planning Officer, Peter Daniel, Heriot-Watt was the new town's greatest lost opportunity.

The next opportunity, pursued vigorously by the Corporation's first Chairman, Sir David Lowe, was even more ambitious. It is perhaps not entirely surprising that he failed to tempt the medical researchers and administrators of the World Health Organisation to the green fields of Livingston rather than the lakeside city of Geneva. Undeterred, the Corporation continued to pursue ideas commensurate with the potential of the Kirkton site. With Heriot-Watt developing Europe's first Research Park exclusively for research and development organisations at Riccarton, it was a logical extension for Livingston to create the environment for science

Scotland's First Technology Park
Kirkton Campus.

based manufacturing. A liaison committee was set up between the Corporation and Heriot-Watt and Edinburgh Universities to investigate ways in which industry locating on Kirkton Campus could access the local knowledge base.

In 1969, Brigadier Purches gave the green light when he reported to the Board that "owing to the number and nature of enquiries regarding the area of ground marked Kirkton Campus Reserve on the Master Plan, the time was now opportune to prepare it for development." In 1972, the Development Corporation received the final go-ahead from the Scottish Office to start the building programme. Three years later, the Arbrook Division of Ethicon Ltd part of the health care multinational, Johnson & Johnson, became the Campus's first company. Ethicon continues to produce surgical disposables for the world's operating theatres, appropriately from an address in Simpson Parkway, honouring James Young Simpson, the local 19th century pioneer of the use of chloroform as an anaesthetic.

Kirkton Campus was ahead of its time. As initial demand was relatively slow, the Corporation's staff toured the world seeking companies of the right calibre who were seeking a European market base. The accompanying marketing material claimed that, within an hour's drive of six Universities, Kirkton Campus was Europe's best placed industrial location for research orientated industry. The criteria for locating on the Campus were stringent.

Tempting as it might be simply to fill the space, the Corporation remained committed to the concept behind the Campus, whereas many UK developers marketed sites as Technology Parks but accepted all comers. Patience paid off and by the late 1980s, the advanced industries of microelectronics design, pharmaceuticals, medical instrumentation and software were all represented on the Campus. Kirkton was also to become the location for Scotland's first purpose built software centre and its first purpose built Class 4 business accommodation. BSKYB's customer service and subscription handling facility on the Campus was one of the town's fastest growing employers.

Initially, Kirkton Campus extended to 150 acres between the River Almond and the Killandean Burn. By the late 1970s, the strength of demand from high technology sectors led the Corporation to seek approval for the opening up of a further 100 acres to the south. By 1990, with several companies having acquired land for future expansion, the Corporation took the decision to develop a second campus at Eliburn, where the serviced and landscaped site has recently been sold to Scottish Enterprise. This will help to ensure that international technology leaders continue to make it in Livingston.

CAPITAL OF SILICON GLEN

Kirkton Campus was developed by the Corporation at a time when many advanced technology companies from the USA and Japan were seeking an appropriate location for their European operations. Although there are several claims as to who invented the title, Silicon Glen, to describe Scotland's growing strength in microelectronics, by 1980, Livingston could boast with some justification that it was the capital. The town's first electronics company was Sperry-Univac, the US mainframe computer manufacturer, who in 1971 signed the lease on a factory for immediate entry to make computer card punches, only four days after the agreement was negotiated.

Three of Scotland's seven semiconductor companies, NEC, Burr-Brown and Seagate chose to make it in Livingston as well as Shin-Etsu, the UK's only producer of silicon wafers, the industry's raw material. In turn their presence and the town's strategic position close to other microelectronics firms in Central Scotland and the North East of England attracted designers, subcontractors and suppliers from all over the world.

THE OIL INDUSTRY COMES HOME

Microelectronics is only one example of how, by forward planning and keeping an ear to the ground, the Development Corporation aimed from the outset to identify market opportunities as they emerged. Only a few years after the discovery in 1969 of oil in commercial quantities in the North Sea, the Corporation targeted the energy sector. Livingston was, after all, the home of the world's first oil industry and Cameron Iron Works, the town's largest employer, was already moving into the production of forgings for use offshore.

Although Aberdeen became the centre of the new industry because of its proximity to the oil fields, Livingston's ambitions were realised when the oil multinational, Schlumberger chose Deans Industrial Estate for an engineering training centre and the Petroleum Industry Training Board announced the setting up of "the University of Oil." Although the Training Board consolidated its resources in Montrose shortly afterwards, the Livingston facility remained in use as an offshore training centre for many years. Schlumberger's distinctive test rigs still overlook the M8.

For many years, motorway drivers remained unaware that there was a town behind the test rigs. This was resolved by the mid 1990s when the Corporation attracted one of its last property developments, the Fairways Business Park. Now a Travelodge hotel, a service station and several offices have provided a gateway to Livingston from the M8.

NEW SKILLS FOR NEW INDUSTRIES

The importance of a significant training resource for the town was always recognised, both to retrain workers from older industries such as heavy

Capital of Silicon Glen
Skill and an appropriate environment for technology combined to make Livingston capital of Silicon Glen. Its microelectronics portfolio includes not only Seagate but Burr-Brown, NEC and Shin-Etsu Handotai while its broader electronics community includes Bull, Dynamic Imaging, Jabil Circuits, Mitsubishi, Schindler, Seiko Instruments, SEEL and Techdyne.

Pioneering New Skills
To ensure that the skills of young people matched the needs of modern industry, Information Technology Centres were established throughout the UK. Livingston was the home of the West Lothian ITEC, the first in Scotland, which also managed the Scottish network. It was visited in 1983 by Kenneth Baker, then Minister for Information Technology.

engineering and to meet the skills needs of incoming industry. In the late 1960s, the Corporation successfully put up a vigorous fight to attract MOTEC, the UK's second multi-disciplinary residential training centre for the transport industry. Located on a 5 acre site within Deans Industrial Estate, MOTEC has since trained many thousands of apprentices.

With strong support from local employers, West Lothian College increasingly provided courses for the training of engineering apprentices and electronics technicians in a series of temporary locations in Livingston. From the early 1980s, the Corporation's role in managing the training of hundreds of young or unemployed residents through the Manpower Services Commission programmes also helped to increase the skills base especially among smaller businesses. Around 90% of trainees went on to find employment.

SELLING LIVINGSTON TO THE WORLD

One of the reasons why new towns were particularly successful in attracting new industry was their pioneering approach to marketing and to handling the resulting business enquiries at a time when local authorities were only just beginning to recognise the importance of economic development.

It is easy to forget that a Japanese manager's understanding of Scotland is likely to be as limited as the Scots' knowledge of Osaka. In attracting overseas companies, therefore, the first objective was to sell Scotland and only then to market individual locations within it. In helping to make the case for Scotland, Livingston Development Corporation staff worked closely with the national organisations entrusted with the task: the Scottish Office, the Scottish Council Development and Industry, the Scottish Development Agency and for the last fifteen years, Locate in Scotland.

Within the UK, the emphasis was different with the Corporation directly targeting firms in the often overheated economy of the South East of England or those operating in key sectors such as electronics and health care. In order to share the high costs of marketing and provide a base from which to tackle industrialists reluctant to travel North until they were convinced of the benefits, in 1973, the Scottish new towns jointly opened an office in the heart of London.

Every possible marketing tactic was used in putting Livingston on the international map. Staff manned stands at the world's leading electronics, health care and oil exhibitions, and knocked on the doors of the multinationals. Countless brochures, videos and information packs were designed, putting forward the case for making it in Livingston, including in 1973, the first promotional document in Japanese produced by a Scottish new town.

If a company expressed an interest in Livingston, however tentative, all the stops were pulled out. When, in 1974, George Whiley, the printing foil manufacturers were considering moving their whole operation out of the South East, the Development Corporation gave presentations within the company's Croydon headquarters to tempt key staff to make the move North. They were then invited to Livingston to see for themselves.

A varied stock of housing was reserved to meet the needs of incoming staff. When a company came to inspect the new town, the Corporation's limousine would be waiting at the airport. A welcome from a Board member in Howden Park Centre would be followed by a tour of the town, exploring possible sites and meeting top management from some of the companies already established in the town.

If first impressions proved positive, a period of intense and complex negotiation followed, covering everything from site preparation to meetings with possible financial backers. In a highly competitive environment, with several countries or regions bidding for a project, success was by no means guaranteed Once the final decision to make it in Livingston had been taken, most companies wanted to move in as quickly as possible. The Corporation's architects and engineers worked with company personnel on the design or adaptation of their new factory while staff in the Estates and Marketing Department answered the myriad of questions which arose especially if the company was new to Britain.

After the operation opened for business, the Corporation's staff remained in close touch to smooth out any teething troubles and to be ready when the company wanted to expand. Livingston was quick to recognise that its goal of employment creation could be met as much from helping existing companies to grow as from wooing new investors.

International investors are often criticised for moving out if there is a downturn in their market or their machinery needs upgrading. In line with all new towns, Livingston had its casualties including Unisys, Sperry-Univac and Pye-TMC. Two of Livingston's most ambitious ventures, in persuading US technology experts to set up their first production operation in Livingston failed in the short term. Both Damon Biotech, Scotland's first overseas investment in biotechnology and Integrated Power Semiconductors, for whom the Development Corporation raised finance

Industrial Show Case
Opened in 1972 by Lord Polwarth, Minister of State at the Scottish Office, the LINDEX exhibition which attracted 5,000 visitors, played a critical role in attracting the attention of industry and the media to the new town's potential. Its success spurred the Board briefly to consider a permanent industrial exhibition site.

Brucefield Industrial Park

on the commercial market, succumbed to financial difficulties in the States.

IPS, however, was bought by Seagate Technology which continues to make power semiconductors, the essential components of computer disk drives in Livingston. The third US entrepreneur to choose Livingston turned out to be a winner. Intelligent Applications Ltd, the company established by the ex-Pentagon scientist, Dr Robert Milne, has won the town's first Queen's Award for Technology with his expert systems software.

FAST RUNNING OUT OF SPACE

As early as 1973, the Corporation was running out of serviced industrial land for its advance factory building programme. There were two possible areas for expansion, Linhouse/Williamston to the south and Brucefield, at the extreme south west corner of the town. Both pieces of land lay outside the new town's designated area. The Corporation's preferred choice was Linhouse, because of its location and greater potential for rapid development. Negotiations with Midlothian County Council to purchase the Linhouse site broke down, however, at the last moment.

After the local government reorganisation of 1975 and a review of industrial accommodation by Lothian Regional Council, the Linhouse opportunity was lost.

The Corporation, therefore, fell back on the option of developing Brucefield and a smaller piece of land at Williamston, both of which it already owned. These were brought into the designated area by 1978. After part of the Brucefield estate was deemed unsuitable if a clear boundary between Livingston and the neighbouring village of Polbeth was to be preserved, site work started for 20 advance factories on what was to become Brucefield Industrial Park in 1977. Brucefield proved very popular with light industry from electronics to double glazing, and each of the next few years was marked by a further phase of the development of the Park. Like Kirkton Campus before it, Brucefield set new standards in industrial design and landscaping.

Several further approaches were made to develop Linhouse by the Corporation who disagreed with its reservation by Lothian Regional Council as a site suitable for a very large single user, reflecting the national planning view of the time. Although Livingston was unable to accommodate Motorola when it sought a large site for its cellular phone plant in the early 1990s, the Corporation helped to ensure that the company located on nearby land owned by the Scottish Development Agency at Easter Inch. Motorola was also provided with temporary accommodation by the Corporation on Brucefield Industrial Park until its new facility was built. Motorola demonstrated the role envisaged for Livingston in the Lothian Regional Survey of the mid 1960s, namely that in acting as a magnet for industry, the town would provide spin-off benefits to the wider local economy.

WELCOMING THE JAPANESE

The final proof of the Development Corporation's successful approach to economic development, was demonstrated with the arrival of the Japanese in order to manufacture within the tariff-free zone of the European Community. The first Japanese company to move in was Hitachi which set up a Scottish distribution centre for its consumer goods in 1978. This was followed in 1979, by one of the most significant events in the development of the town's economy, the announcement by NEC that it was to establish a semiconductor plant, persuaded by Livingston's emerging role as capital of Silicon Glen. With its most recent expansion programme, NEC has committed nearly three quarters of a billion pounds to its Livingston operation, one of the largest investments ever made by a Japanese company in Europe. It is now the town's largest industrial employer with 1,350 staff and in 1995, acquired additional land for future expansion.

In 1983, the same year as the Queen formally opened NEC's facility on the Deans Industrial Estate, Shin-Etsu Handotai decided to establish a silicon wafer production plant in Livingston and Mitsubishi opened a temporary factory to manufacture video cassette recorders. The market for these new consumer goods took off so rapidly that the Development Corporation staff had to work flat out to ensure that the company's production did not fall behind demand. Records were broken when the 100,000 sq ft factory was opened within three months of Mitsubishi's decision to locate in Livingston. The company has since expanded on five occasions.

The Japanese companies have not only brought jobs and wealth to Livingston but have added a touch of the exotic to the life of a town which has welcomed businesses from over 20 countries. Special efforts were made by Corporation staff and residents to make the overseas visitors feel at home, whether by helping to arrange a Saturday school for Japanese children or simply by inviting them into their houses. The benefits have been mutual. The new families introduced Livingston to the cookery of their countries through the International Club at

Value Added
Japanese companies have brought to Livingston not only investment of close to £1bn but also their own colourful traditions and customs.

The World of Livingston

Just as Livingston has attracted companies like W L Gore and the Cubix Corporation from over twenty countries, Livingston itself is part of the international map. There is: Livingston, Alabama • Livingston, Guatemala • Livingston, Kentucky • Livingston, Louisiana • Livingston, Montana • Livingston, New York State • Livingston, South Carolina • Livingston,. Scotland • Livingston, Tennessee • Livingston, Texas • Livingston, Wisconsin

Craigs Farm and to their culture during Festivals and special occasions.

Perhaps the most memorable and certainly the most moving official visit to Livingston, a town accustomed to being inspected by Dutch planners or African civil servants, was by the Chiba Boys and Girls choir. No language barrier could restrain the spontaneity and laughter as the Japanese made friends with the children of Livingston.

LIVINGSTON SAYS NO

It is in the nature of the new town to welcome international business. On one occasion, however, Livingston said no. After months of negotiation with the Estates and Marketing Department, in late 1984, Union Carbide, the US chemicals company, chose Livingston in preference to a number of other sites in Europe for a new gas mixing plant for the semiconductor industry to employ around 70 people. The company already had a sales office in the town. The one problem was that the manufacturing process involved the transport and use of the potentially dangerous compound, arsene.

The Development Corporation had authorised a number of safety and environmental checks before taking a final decision on planning permission and started to buy in the materials for the new factory. Before the checks were completed, however, the news broke of an explosion at Union Carbide's Bhopal fertiliser plant in India, resulting in both immediate and longer term casualties. The company saw no need for concern, as the Livingston plant would be producing a different product and would be designed to meet the stringent standards of UK and European Community legislation. When the news came out, however, the town reacted very differently.

An action group, LACE, was swiftly formed They organised two public meetings which attracted so many people that they had to be relayed by television to those who could not get into the hall. The message from these meetings was clear and simple: Livingston residents did not want the Union Carbide plant. For the first and only time in the Corporation's history, the Chairman called an emergency Board meeting. After debating the options, the Board resolved to refuse planning permission, in respect for the "genuine fears and concerns of the residents of Livingston."

Although from the Corporation's point of view, the decision meant protracted dealings with a very unhappy company, the public response to Union Carbide's plans showed above all that the town was growing up. The people of Livingston were prepared to rise to the defence of what they saw as a threat to their town.

THE BUSINESS OF SERVICE

Given the need to achieve an employment balance split between manufacturing and service industries, an early priority was to develop accommodation for office use. In 1970 in response to growing demand, the Board decided to release the site originally designated for a car showroom in Craigshill for a two storey office block, Shiel House. A second development, Peel House in Ladywell shortly followed. Six of the thirteen tenants of Shiel House were sales offices of electronics firms including the US computer manufacturer, Digital Equipment who was looking to establish a Scottish sales office for its popular PDP11 minicomputers. In 1996, Digital set up a software design and support centre in Lauder House, the Corporation's last speculative office development, on the new Almondvale Business Park.

In the early 1970s, the Corporation solved the problem of accommodation for tradesmen such as plumbers and decorators and small manufacturers by converting spare garages in Craigshill into workshops. This proved so popular that more garages were converted as well as the construction of purpose-built service units in districts such as Knightsridge and Dedridge. In the mid 1990s, the Estates and Marketing Department even promoted building plots in Kirkton for small professional firms who wished to design and build their own offices.

In order to achieve its employment targets, however, the Corporation had to seek out large office employers. In considering its own accommodation needs, the Government was supportive of the Scottish new towns' aspirations to provide a range of employment opportunities for their residents. East Kilbride got the Centre 1 tax office, Cumbernauld, the PAYE centre and in 1972, Livingston was chosen for the administration of social security benefits for Scotland and the North of England. In 1985, the town had a visit from the taxman when the Inland Revenue established an on-line processing centre to handle the tax affairs of parts of London and Northern Ireland.

One Government agency which eventually did not come despite an expression of serious interest was the Scottish Special Housing Association, responsible for augmenting local authority housing. In 1972, it entered into discussions with the Development Corporation about moving its headquarters from Edinburgh where the organisation operated from 17 different offices. Although hopes ran high and negotiations were lengthy, the Association eventually decided not to leave the capital.

Satellite Centre
One of the town's fastest growing operations, Sky Subscriber Services employs 1,400 people on Kirkton Campus while the office complexes in Almondvale house a variety of service activity from insurance to electronics distribution. Pentland House, one of the town's first office blocks looked to passing aircraft to communicate its message.

Livingston's Largest Inward Investment
NEC represents one of the largest investments by a Japanese company in Europe. "Our Livingston factory is one of the most productive semiconductor plants in the world, thanks largely to the skills and enthusiasm of our workforce."
Toshio Nakamura, Managing Director, NEC Semiconductors (UK) Ltd

Major offices were seen as a key component of the town centre and in the early 1980s, the Corporation took the bold step of building its own town centre office blocks on a speculative basis backed by commercial funding. Located to the north and south of the shopping centre, these were named after ranges of Scottish hills. When Sidlaw House proved relatively slow to let, it provided the Development Corporation with the solution to a problem of its own, the shortage of space within its headquarters in Livingston Village. The Corporation's staff moved into four floors of Sidlaw House, selling their previous headquarters to a private developer to be subdivided into small suites as Kirkton Business Centre.

TARGETS EXCEEDED

The establishment of West Lothian Council in the Corporation's former headquarters within Almondvale in 1995 marked a fitting conclusion to the Development Corporation's involvement in stimulating the town's economic growth. The transfer of over 200 Council staff contributed to a new record of over 4,000 jobs created in Livingston in the last year of the Development Corporation's life This was four times the annual target set in the Master Plan. Although there have been difficult times, notably during the early 1980s when worldwide recession was combined with the closure of some of the town's firms which were unable to make the switch from a labour to a technology based mode of operation, the town's employment curve has been consistently upwards. Over the last sixteen years, the target of averaging 1,000 new jobs a year has been maintained.

There are a number of reasons why Livingston has exceeded its planners' projections in terms of economic development. Some of these date back to Livingston's foundations as the first UK new town to be designated as a growth centre, a policy which has clearly stood the test of time. Although dictated by necessity, the choice of site was inspired, sufficiently far from the capital not to be overshadowed by it but sufficiently close for companies to benefit from contact with its educational, research and financial communities. Proximity to national and international transport hubs was matched by a young workforce and a good financial deal.

The Corporation's contribution lay in its ability to offer a virtually one-door approach to businesses which decided to make it in Livingston. The Corporation could offer a site or a factory, design expertise, planning permission and loan finance, a package which gave Livingston a competitive edge in the pursuit of international investment.

8
A NEW HOUSE IN A NEW TOWN

Even more than a job, it was the prospect of a house which decided most families to move to Livingston. In the 1960's, pressure on housing was intense, at a time when much of the housing stock was old and poorly maintained. Post-War prosperity and the baby boom had raised aspirations. The younger generation wanted to start out married life in their own house equipped with all the latest labour saving devices rather than move in with their parents. They wished their children to enjoy what their own upbringing in a Glasgow tenement or miner's row lacked: fresh air, a safe place to play and a clean, healthy environment

1,000 HOUSES A YEAR

The Master Plan envisaged a mix of houses including terraces, maisonettes and flats, the majority designed for families with most having their own garden, patio or private space. High standards in house design, adequate heating and insulation were considered to be essential. Half the homes were to have their own garage and the rest to be provided with off-street parking. Because of shortage of land, housing densities were high especially in districts close to the centre of the town.

Fortunately for Livingston, the Master Plan target of 1,000 houses a year for the next two decades proved an unrealisable ambition. By 1971, the house building programme was averaging two thirds of the annual target and in the years 1972-76, only an average of 570 houses a year were built, although for a few years thereafter, the targets were met or even exceeded. At times, however, finding tenants proved to be hard work.

Meanwhile, land was at an ever scarcer premium. The town's economic success meant that more land had to be zoned for industry than the Master Plan envisaged. Relaxation in Government housing cost rules allowed for lower densities of housing leading to a more attractive and informal layout of Corporation housing. Private developers, who became increasingly active in the 1980s also designed to much lower densities. It became increasingly clear that Livingston simply did not have the land available to accommodate 70,000 people.

THE FIRST HOUSES

In 1962, the Board agreed to the Secretary of

I Declare This Factory....
The formal opening of Laing's factory hinted at problems to come. When the Government Minister pressed the button which was to start the concrete flowing, nothing happened. Half an hour passed amid growing embarrassment until the machinery could be persuaded to respond. Nearly two decades later, the first tenants moved back into the, by now completely refurbished, "piano blocks."

Blow the House Down
The first arrivals on the scene of devastation during the great gale of 1968 were the Ministers who lived in Craigshill. They did what they could to comfort the residents who had lost their roofs. By the end of the next day, all the tenants who needed to be rehoused had a key to a new house. The following morning, a convoy of 19 furniture vans ferried their possessions to their new home. Meanwhile, a group of children gathered round one of the devastated houses, chanting " he huffed and he puffed and he blew the house down."

State's initial target that 200 houses should be available for workers for the expanding Bathgate tractor plant "at regular intervals" from June 1964, as well as deciding to provide 400 houses for Corporation staff, building workers and the employees of incoming firms. An almost immediate start was made in Livingston Station.

Although the first houses were built by traditional methods, the only way that 1,000 houses a year could be achieved was by using industrial systems. Although, with hindsight these systems had serious drawbacks, they offered a way of getting round the severe shortages of materials and labour experienced in the 1960s building boom. Applying technology in a bold and confident way was part of the "brave new world".

Industrial methods meant that houses were put together from a series of concrete panels, slotted together to form the shell. In 1964 after reviewing over twelve such systems, Jespersen was selected. The UK agent for this Danish design was John Laing, the national building contractor who erected a factory in Livingston to serve the Scottish market. On the strength of the Livingston contract, Laings also supplied Jespersen designs for other local authorities and new towns including 500 in Glenrothes.

Most of the Jerpersen houses consisted of two stories of flats with a maisonette above. Despite the rigours of the Scottish climate, they reflected the obsession of the time with balconies, being built as a set of steps with the balcony of one house forming the living room ceiling of the house below. The flats soon earned the nickname of the "piano blocks". The layout of the housing in regimented blocks along the contours of Craigshill was dictated by the need to create room for the tower cranes lifting the prefabricated concrete blocks into place.

Because of the pressure to build quickly and cheaply, the Livingston variant of the Jespersen system, designed by the Corporation's architects, was built untested. Jespersen was not the only industrialised building system to be used. Part of Craigshill was built using the Costain Siporex system which needed remedial work to combat dampness as early as 1969 and Bett Bison flats encountered similar problems. The Skarne system was tested in a small pilot scheme at Livingston Station.

WIND AND WATER TIGHT?

Problems with the design of the Jespersen flats started to emerge before the contract was completed with the construction programme itself hindered by a number of technical problems. When the wind blew in certain directions, it drove rain on to the balconies where it gathered and seeped into the room below. Disaster struck on the night of 15th January, 1968, when a hurricane travelled across Central Scotland bringing devastation in its wake. The roofs of 68 houses in Craigshill blew off and many families had to be rehoused. An investigation into the damage revealed deeper problems: badly made and badly installed components and weak points in fittings where damp had crept in.

Even after the immediate storm damage was repaired, rain penetration remained a serious problem. After a sustained local campaign, the Development Corporation decided at its 100th Board meeting in February 1969 to take comprehensive, corrective action. Because of uncertainty as to the efficacy of the proposed treatment, one block was to be tackled as a pilot. Ironically, the contract was won by the lowest of eight tenderers, John Laing Construction, the firm which had built the original flats. The pilot successfully withstood the weather of the winter of 1969 and the go ahead was given to tackle the other nineteen blocks at a total cost of £350,000.

Thus early in its life, the Corporation had to work out a policy for decanting 400 tenants while the 18 month repair programme was carried out. A stockpile of new houses was built up and tenants were given the choice of a permanent move or temporary rehousing until their old home was repaired. From 1969, the Jespersen saga moved into the law courts with claim and counterclaim made against the contractor. The dispute was eventually settled out of court in the Corporation's favour during 1984 by which time the "piano blocks" were undergoing a further transformation.

THE VOLUME YEARS

Despite the early teething problems, Craigshill built up fairly rapidly to its target population of 10,000. Howden, Ladywell and Knightsridge were started in the late 1960s and Dedridge and Deans followed in the early 1970s. The volume years of Corporation house building peaked in the late 1970s, with the target of 1,000 houses a year exceeded on several occasions.

In the early 1970s, although the Corporation reverted to traditional building methods, tight budgets and the necessary speed of building increasingly constrained design in districts like Ladywell and Howden. Whereas at one time the Scottish new towns were required to build housing to a higher standard than private contractors, this distinction was gradually eroded by growing Government concern over costs. Particular difficulties were experienced in Dedridge, where

Partnerships
Tackling the problems of Knightsridge brought together the Corporation, the local authorities, health professionals, community workers, the police and local people to deliver an integrated programme of area renewal. The approach typified the Corporation's core philosophy and way of working in partnership with others, whether in building roads or seeking overseas investment.

Providing accommodation for the town's older citizens was a growing priority

1,000 houses were planned to be built between 1972-78. Partly with a view to achieving economies of scale, all the contracts were let to the one building firm. Unable to cope with a very large commitment which included other new towns and local authorities, the company failed in 1973 leaving large parts of Dedridge fenced off while the liquidators resolved the bankruptcy.

One area of Knightsridge was designed by Scottish Development Department architects in the early 1970s to show that it was possible to build attractive low rise and low cost, housing in high densities on a north facing slope. Houses, however, were so tightly packed that most views were straight into the neighbour's windows. Because of noise, cold and confined space, this part of Knightsridge proved very difficult to let for several years. This in turn led to other problems: vandalism, a concentration of families with limited employment opportunities, petty crime. Such problems were by no means unique to the new towns. When the volume of tenants' complaints and the results of the 1981 Census revealed the extent of Knightsridge's difficulties, the Corporation took appropriate action to tackle the complex and interwoven set of issues to which the original design had contributed.

From the mid 1970s, with a more sympathetic Government approach to costs, the design and layout of new housing districts such as Knightsridge West and Deans East, placed greater emphasis on amenity and space and redefined the relationship people and cars. Most later residential districts consisted of traditional harled terraced houses set in small groups which provided a sense of identity while retaining a degree of privacy. Although they may not have been as architecturally dramatic as some of the estates built in other new towns, the design of Livingston's housing was generally popular with tenants, as was shown in house sales when the Right to Buy legislation came into force.

The Development Corporation's house building programme virtually stopped in its tracks during the early 1980s following the Government's national moratorium on publicly financed new housing. The town was to see a final major burst of Corporation house building in the early 1990s when the moratorium was relaxed in the face of strong demand for rented accommodation from second generation residents. In its last years, the Corporation built 450 new houses in Eliburn and Ladywell, handing them over on completion to a housing association, as well as encouraging private house builders to address the market for rented accommodation.

HELPING RESIDENTS TO HELP THEMSELVES

In the lean years of the moratorium, the one exception to the ban on new public housing was expenditure on accommodation for people with special needs. The expectation in most new towns was that housing for older residents was not needed for at least the first twenty years Livingston was different. Although, a very young town, the town had the unusual distinction of having within its boundaries one of Scotland's most elderly communities, in Livingston Station. In 1973, the town's first sheltered housing, Restondene, was opened in Deans, with accommodation for 25 residents, a warden and a common room. This marked a move away from the traditional approach of housing the elderly in large institutions to providing an atmosphere which was as close to home as possible. A second sheltered housing development, Craigengar, was built in Craigshill in 1990 while in later districts like Dedridge, where Lothian Regional Council also built a home for the elderly at Crofthead, space near central amenities was reserved for single storey housing for older residents.

Meeting the needs of individuals with special housing requirements was a Corporation priority long before the current emphasis on care in the community. In many cases, it simply meant adapting an existing house to accommodate a wheel chair or a kidney machine. Corporation staff also worked closely with specialist housing associations such as Margaret Blackwood, Hanover, Kirk Care and Ark to build accommodation designed for people who needed a greater degree of support. In 1973, the first purpose built home for mentally handicapped children opened and in 1982, the YMCA and Link Housing Association converted flats in Craigshill to provide a hostel for homeless teenagers Even in its last year of operation, the Corporation was building four houses for people moving out of the local Gogarburn hospital.

FINDING PEOPLE FOR THE HOUSES

In the early years, Livingston operated a very strict house letting policy, with priority given to people who had a job in the town or who were nominated through Glasgow's overspill programme. By the end of the 1960s, the first surge of demand for housing was beginning to dry up. From 1972, demand received a brief boost from the renewed recruitment drive to take overspill families from West Central Scotland, with vetting procedures being operated much less stringently than before.

Letting garages could also prove difficult. Initially, car ownership was lower than predicted in the Master Plan and many tenants would not or could not pay the additional rental. Faced in places with 60-70% of garages unlet, the Corporation soon reduced

Neighbours

Although in the 1972 Household Survey, residents ranked housing top of thirteen characteristics that they liked about their town, their neighbours attracted strong opinions: "Ladywell is more like a cat and dog home. There are as many pets as there are children." • "The people here do more for their pensioners than any other town." • "Too many workshy men of doubtful honesty with large families are settled in certain areas." • "It used to be like the KGB getting a house in Livingston." • "Applicants should be classified into areas according to education, public morals, housekeeping and attention to civic duties."

its provision of garages to 30% of new housing and eventually only to houses which commanded higher rents. At first tenants were discouraged from erecting their own garages but in 1979 with increasingly severe cuts in the capital budget, this policy was reversed.

Once overspill had formally been abandoned by Glasgow Corporation in 1975, rather than leave houses unlet, it was decided to relax the requirement for tenants to fit the approved categories. Simply going on the waiting list was at times sufficient to secure a house: by 1980, 20% of lettings were to non-priority tenants. Some applicants were very particular, rejecting offer after offer unless they were given a brand new house. For a time, "you can always get a nice, new house in Livingston" became a widely held if erroneous view throughout much of Central Scotland. Efforts were even made to encourage students from Edinburgh's two Universities to take tenancies.

As houses in newer districts became available, tenants especially in the more densely developed areas of Craigshill applied for transfers. Initially, these were often granted leaving some of the older houses unlet for long periods or assigned to people in desperate housing need. "Problem areas" started to build up in certain areas of Craigshill and Knightsridge, where endemic problems with the design and construction of the housing was exacerbated by poverty and its attendant social problems.

Housing problems provided the immediate impetus behind the Knightsridge and Craigshill Initiatives launched by the Corporation in 1986 and 1989, following a period of study and consultation. Rather than simply improving the houses and their immediate environment, the Corporation adopted a much wider strategy, bringing together all the relevant agencies to examine the area as a whole and address the inter-related issues of employment, housing, environment and social facilities.

In parts of Knightsridge, demolition was the only solution to give tenants more space and privacy whereas in Craigshill, apart from the original system built accommodation, much of the housing was by now structurally sound. The solution was to remodel individual blocks of flats to bring them up to modern standards and appearance, although the Scottish Office took some convincing that renewal could be achieved within the costs proposed by the Corporation. In order to introduce a broader range of home ownership, some of the housing was sold to private developers or the growing housing association movement.

LOOKING AFTER ITS OWN

Livingston was the first Scottish new town to recognise that building and letting houses was not enough. New tenants especially in a new town needed help to settle in, to deal with the hundred and one problems from finding a dentist to the money for the next hire purchase instalment and, most important of all, to put down roots. In 1964, the Corporation decided to combine the functions of housing and what it rather quaintly called "social relations", appointing Leslie Higgs, Housing Manager of Glenrothes to the post. Thus, the Corporation was prepared and ready to welcome its first tenants.

The house letting policy had a number of innovative features. In the early years, young families were offered a bedroom additional to their immediate requirements. This not only provided a spare room for visiting relatives but also allowed the family to grow without being faced with the expense and disruption of another move. A team of housing visitors or Arrivals Officers called on new tenants not only to check that they were settling in but with their agreement to gather information about their background and interests. This was then matched with the details of other new arrivals and new residents with common interests put in touch. This unusual form of "dating agency" even resulted in some marriages. As the town became established, welcome committees and neighbourhood networks made up of volunteers helped new residents to feel at home.

The 1970s Household Surveys showed that in general tenants were happy with their houses, although less so with the amenities, or lack of them, in the town. Tenants complaints were those of tenants anywhere: noisy neighbours, delays in repairs, vandalism, unswept snow and rubbish. Some families valued the safety and convenience of having children's play areas close to housing while others complained of the noise and bedrooms being overlooked. A regular complaint from mothers was the lack of a place to put the pram. To address these practical concerns, in the major renewal programmes in Knightsridge and Craigshill, tenants became actively involved in the design process, as well as being surveyed to quantify their likes and dislikes.

When tenants did have problems, they often expected the "Corporation" to deal with them, especially those who came from the cities where until 1975, the local authority "Corporation" looked after items like street lighting and rubbish disposal. On several occasions, Livingston Development Corporation attempted to introduce tenants to the complexities of public life by producing checklists of whom to contact for what. As a new housing district was opened up, a mobile caravan from Housing and Social Relations was among the first arrivals, with staff transferring to a shop or house when it became available.

Paying the rent was a problem for some tenants especially when coupled with the expense of setting up home. New town rents generally were higher than

Ghosts and Garden Fences
Livingston has had its share of unusual tenants. The keys to the first Corporation house were handed over to a couple from Maryhill and their two children by the Lord Provost of Glasgow, Peter Meldrum at 11.30am on the dull, wet morning of 18th November, 1964. The young family were presented with a clock and other gifts amid the popping of press flashlights. The move must have proved too much as the family returned to Glasgow a few months later. In the late 1960s, a house in Howden gained the reputation of being haunted, with mysterious wet footprints, white smears and names disappearing from door plates. Another tenant refused to let the Corporation paint his garden fence until after the town's annual Gardening Competition in case his prize display of honeysuckle was damaged.

Fighting the Damp

As in most post-War estates, condensation and who was responsible for it was a contentious issue in districts like Knightsridge and Craigshill. Many houses were heated by electricity, a low cost energy source until the 1973 Middle East oil crisis. Although the Corporation provided guidance to tenants on how to heat and air their houses effectively, introducing a heat-with-rent scheme in 1980, the cost of heating could present genuine difficulties, especially for tenants new to central heating. In the 1980s, the Corporation's multi-million pound housing renewal programme included installing cavity wall insulation, replacing heating systems and introducing other energy saving measures.

in older Council areas and heating bills were also high especially in houses which suffered from dampness. The Corporation's housing staff devoted considerable energy in devising policies which would make payment of rent as easy as possible as well as helping individual tenants to budget. In 1969, rent stamps were introduced which could be purchased at the Post Office and after the Middle East crisis of 1973, when energy prices soared, Corporation staff devised a number of schemes to help tenants with escalating heating bills. In general, sympathetic housing policies paid off. In the first decade, only eight eviction notices were issued and only three families actually evicted.

A later solution to common problems, whether condensation or vandalism was to set up residents or tenants associations. These gave people a collective voice and made a two way flow of communications with the Development Corporation's staff easier. In the 1980s, tenants associations formed the natural nucleus for the Corporation's policy of actively encouraging tenants to participate in housing matters and to explore different ownership options.

OLDER HOUSING IN A NEW TOWN

By the 1980s, some of the Corporation's housing was showing signs of age. During the moratorium on finance for new housing, the Scottish Office permitted the Corporation to use income from house sales to fund repairs and renewal within its existing stock. In a multi-million pound programme which lasted more than a decade, many houses were given pitched roofs: cladding was replaced and harling brightened up with a distinctive use of colour. Central heating, kitchens and bathrooms were modernised and tumble driers replaced. Gradually, the housing stock was brought up to a uniformly high standard in advance of eventual sale or transfer to a successor landlord.

ACCOMMODATING A BALANCED COMMUNITY

An immediate need was to accommodate those whose work demanded that they lived in the town. As part of the original package to attract industry, the Corporation built higher rent, executive housing, which proved popular with company managers and helped at a time of national shortages to attract teachers to the town's new schools.

As well as speculative private housing, other initiatives were launched by the Corporation to widen the range of accommodation available in the town. Housing associations were encouraged to build in the town, in order to broaden the options available to residents and a fruitful partnership developed between the Corporation and several associations, who provided a range of special needs accommodation. This approach of working alongside housing associations from an early date was brought to its logical conclusion when the Corporation's own housing staff formed the Almond Housing Association.

From an early stage, the Development Corporation was willing to sell its houses to residents although this was not actively marketed. Following legislation in the early 1970s, the Corporation took a more active stance in offering its houses for sale. Leaflets were delivered to all households by teams of local Scouts and Guides telling them of the benefits of buying their own home and outlining the necessary procedures. 4,000 houses of 123 different types from 1 bedroom bungalows to 6-7 bedroom houses were available for sale including an area of Craigshill, where houses were set aside when they became vacant. Priority in house sales was given to existing residents with sitting tenants being offered a £300 discount. The Corporation itself could provide loans on a discretionary basis for tenants who had been turned down by their building society.

A much more vigorous drive towards home ownership came less than a decade later with the Tenants Rights etc (Scotland) Act of 1980 giving local authority and Development Corporation tenants the right to buy their home with substantial discounts. The former Housing Manager, Leslie Higgs described this as "the Sale of the Century." Again, the Corporation actively encouraged its tenants to take up the option.

A HOME OF ONE'S OWN

Although right from the start unlike some new towns, Livingston Development Corporation had recognised the role of private housing in achieving its goal of a balanced community, like most new towns it found this initially difficult to put into practice. Through to the mid 1970s, almost the only success had been a small development in Livingston Village and a very positive take-up of individual plots at Murieston and Woodlands Park. A site in Knightsridge, won in a design competition in 1972, was very slow to get started.

The initial spur to development came with the launch of the Corporation's combined golf course and housing package where homes by Rush & Tompkins were started in 1978 as part of a 600 house development. In the next few years, there were to be other sporadic bursts of interest with private house building in Livingston Village, Murieston and Deans.

A Balanced Community
In 1981, when owner occupation stood at 12%, the Board agreed a major policy initiative to encourage private house building, extending its highly successful approach in industrial development to housing. Specific measures included:
- *Creating a bank of sites throughout the town with distinctive features to attract different market sectors including volume builders.*
- *Offering flexible financial arrangements to builders.*
- *Marketing Livingston as a desirable place to live.*
- *Continuing to oppose planning applications for major housing developments on unzoned sites near Livingston.*

By the early 1980s, the Corporation recognised the need for a more concerted and corporate approach to the encouragement of private house building in the town. The main ingredients of the resulting strategy were an intensive marketing campaign both to developers and their potential customers, the attraction of volume builders through the provision of large sites with simplified briefs, the identification of special sites where significantly high standards would be adhered to and guarantees of continuity of sites to builders who demonstrated their commitment to develop in Livingston. An additional catalyst to Livingston's gaining credibility with private house builders came with the opening of the town's two railway stations in the mid 1980s making commuting to the capital a twenty minute journey.

Despite the scepticism of the Scottish House Builders Federation that these measures would be sufficient to allow the Corporation to achieve its target of 250 and ultimately 300 private house completions a year, the number of builders active in the town steadily increased throughout the 1980s from around five to over twenty. The first target was passed and the second exceeded by the Corporation's last year of operation. By the early 1990s, estate agents reported healthy and growing interest in the town, with houses at the top end of the market commanding prices over £200,000. At last, Livingston was a "desirable area".

As late as 1980, the Corporation owned 90% of the town's housing. Within the next 16 years, home ownership rose dramatically to its present position of over 60% A sign of a maturing town must be that its residents want to secure a stake in its future.

9
DOWN YOUR WAY

In the Master Plan, access and catchment area were the main criteria used to assign facilities such as shops and community centres for Livingston's residential areas. The objectives were that no young child should have to walk more than a quarter of a mile to school whereas a larger local shopping centre was only to be allocated when the population which it was to serve was close to the target of 10,000-15,000. Tenants' meeting places were to be provided for every 400-500 households.

In this, Livingston differed from most previous new towns where planning was based on the concept of neighbourhoods, each with its shops, health services and other resources. In many ways, it followed the natural evolution of older towns where new facilities are provided only when the population justifies them.

As the town developed, practical considerations often confirmed the logic of the planner's model although changing population estimates, budget cuts and commercial demands influenced the final shape of Craigshill and Howden, Knightsridge and Deans. They demonstrated the need for flexibility which the Master Plan had built in from the start. The Corporation's policy could occasionally cause friction with community activists who naturally campaigned for their district to have the same resources as the one next door.

In planning its districts, the Corporation was largely dependent on the resources and goodwill of other organisations. In many aspects, it was extremely fortunate in the pioneering and forward looking approach that its partners took to the new town. Regarding Livingston as the appropriate place in which to test out new ideas, education authorities, Churches and the health services declared their faith in the new town by putting in resources in advance of need.

JUGGLING THE SCHOOL ROLLS

Education was originally planned on the basis of three primary schools feeding into a secondary school. Craigshill, the first new district to be built, followed this model. The new town's first primary school, Riverside, built by Midlothian County Council to accommodate 600 pupils, opened on Monday 25th April, 1966 with three pupils, a headmaster and a janitor. Two of the pupils were the children of the town's first GP, Dr Barker. Letham and Almondbank Primaries quickly followed as the population grew.

"We confidently expect that Craigshill will prove to be a model of compact urban development which will successfully meet the needs of the motor age."
Corporation Annual Report 1965

First 2 Last
The earliest school Riverside Primary was also the birthplace of the Ecumenical Experiment while the last school St. Margaret's R.C. Secondary shares its pool with the town's swimming clubs.

Meanwhile, the existing primary school at Livingston Station served the new residents of Deans. By 1966, with the school roll close to 250, the school was bursting at the seams and huts were erected in the playground to serve as temporary classrooms. The headmaster toured the new houses, to see if he could find an extra teacher. Three years later, with the roll now standing at over 300, teachers and pupils moved into Deans Primary School, the second to be built by West Lothian County Council. The first by a few months was Knightsridge, only the second school of its particular design in Scotland.

Keeping pace with the population was a major challenge for the education authorities in the early 1970s. Toronto Primary, the first school to open in Howden was "bulging at the seams from the day it opened. With Harrysmuir Primary in neighbouring Ladywell not scheduled to come on stream for another two years, parents campaigned for action and education officials dreaded the start of each new term. As an emergency measure, overspill classes were housed in Craigshill High School.

Until the town's first secondary school opened in 1969, senior pupils were bussed to West Calder High School, causing considerable parental concern in the dark winter mornings. Built at a cost of £1m next to the Shopping Mall, Craigshill High took the form of a figure of eight with one five storey courtyard opening on to a pedestrian forecourt and a smaller enclosed court. A covered way provided access to the swimming pool and indoor sports facilities. Outdoor sport, however, presented more of a problem. Because of the need to ensure land for housing in the centre of Craigshill, the playing fields were located more than half a mile from the school. Much of the games period was spent en route from classroom to pitch.

When it opened, Craigshill High had 120 pupils, the headmaster, James Pirie, and seven teachers. For the next ten years, Craigshill High was to be the only secondary school for the Midlothian part of the town, becoming increasingly overcrowded as the population grew. When Inveralmond Community High School finally opened in 1979, Craigshill High had 1,500 pupils and 100 teachers.

Inveralmond had a complex history. At the beginning of 1972, Midlothian County Council dropped a bombshell. Instead of the planned secondary school for Roman Catholic pupils in Howden, a super high school was to be built for 2,000 pupils from Craigshill, Howden and Ladywell, with the existing Craigshill High becoming the Roman Catholic secondary school. The pros and cons of such a large school were widely debated by parents and educational experts alike. In mid 1973, plans for the "super school" were abandoned owing to a severe cutback in Midlothian's education budget but after a showdown meeting with the Minister of State for Health and Education, the plans were reprieved.

When Lothian Regional Council took over responsibility for education in 1975, the plans were modified to cater for a roll of 1,600 serving Ladywell and Howden. The school was provided with a swimming pool, theatre workshop, squash courts and cafe for community use.

Inveralmond was not the town's first community school. The first schools in the early districts were used for many purposes, initially out of necessity. Riverside Primary served as youth centre, Church, cinema, community meeting hall and a dormitory for the Almondell summer work camps while Almondbank included a library and adult education facilities and Deans Primary doubled up as a GP's surgery.

This experience of using schools for a whole range of community activities may have given West Lothian's Education Committee the confidence to sanction an even bolder experiment Although generally more traditional and conservative as a Council than Midlothian, West Lothian was responsible for introducing Scotland's first community school at Deans, opened in 1978, a few months earlier than Midlothian's Inveralmond. The idea of adults joining children in the classroom was so novel that some teachers had to be brought in from areas of England which had pioneered this approach.

Providing schools for Roman Catholic children posed a problem for many years. Although as part of the ecumenical movement, hopes were expressed that schools would be strictly non-denominational, this was not to be. In the early years, however, children from all faiths had to share school accommodation out of necessity.

The first fifty Catholic primary school pupils were bussed to East Calder until a vigorous campaign by parents, concerned at the rigours of winter travel, forced Midlothian County Council to provide them with an annexe at Letham Primary school in 1969. By the early 1970s, 600 RC primary pupils were taught in Craigshill High along with overspill from Howden. Craigshill's surplus accommodation was fast diminishing, as the roll broke the 1,000 mark. The first RC primary, St Andrews, finally opened in Howden in 1972.

Ironically, Livingston finally achieved its Roman Catholic secondary school because of falling school

The Clochemerle of Craigshill

In 1969, the Corporation sold Midlothian County Council a site for a public toilet, for £25.and a penny. When the £6,000 convenience opened, it had no attendant. The Corporation's Chairman made headlines when he suggested that for a quality convenience, residents should be willing to pay 6d rather than the customary penny. In 1972, after refurbishing the toilets, the Council announced that unlike other conveniences Craigshill would close at 6pm. The next year, it climbed down and with a fresh coat of paint, the toilet reopened on a 24 hour basis. The saga moved Councillor Hoey to remark "the Taj Mahal could have been built for the same price." Meanwhile, the Corporation courageously considered new toilets for Howden and Almondvale. Craigshill's Clochemerle is still operational today, a monument to perseverance.

rolls. In the early 1980s, not long after the opening of James Young High School in Dedridge, Lothian Regional Council conducted a major review of school provision. A site which had been earmarked for a non-denominational high school in Eliburn was surplus to requirements.

This review offered the final solution to Roman Catholic secondary education in the town, with the building of the elegant St Margaret's Secondary school on the Northern slopes of the Almond valley in Howden West, the Eliburn site being deemed insufficiently central. It also marked a very different set of priorities from the early years. With school rolls plummeting, Livingston only gained St Margaret's at the expense of two other secondary schools, Bathgate's St Mary's and Our Lady's in Broxburn as almost all West Lothian's needs could be served by the new Livingston school and St Kentigern's in Blackburn.

The town too suffered its own closure with Craigshill High, its roll now down to 300, being declared surplus to requirements. A concerted campaign failed to save the school itself from demolition in 1995 but rescued its sports facilities for community use.

FROM ONE GP TO ST JOHNS

Livingston's first doctor, Dr Barker initially held his surgery from a house in Broom Walk, Craigshill, until the Craigshill Health Centre opened in 1969. Like many community resources in Livingston, a new town environment inspired innovation and experimentation. Craigshill was one of Scotland's first neighbourhood health centres and one of the first integrated practices in the country, providing residents with access to dental, nursing and community health care as well as the services of three GPs. The Wednesday afternoon ante-natal clinic was said to be Livingston's most popular social club of the early 1970s.

The Craigshill Health Centre was chosen to pioneer several of the new initiatives being considered for the management of health care provision in Scotland. In the Livingston Project, the Health Services Joint Advisory Group for Livingston co-ordinated the work of the six authorities responsible for health care in the area. In order to address growing national difficulties in attracting doctors to general practice, it experimented with the idea of GP specialists in hospitals. As well as normal practice duties within the community, the GP became a consultant in a specific branch of medicine such as paediatrics. In the move to computerising the administration of health services, the Scottish Office also chose the Craigshill Health Centre to pilot the keeping of patient records on computer and a system to recall young patients for booster injections.

In 1972 a temporary centre was opened for Howden and Ladywell followed in 1981 by permanent health centres in Carmondean and Dedridge to serve the more outlying districts. Until the mid 1980s, when deregulation was acceptd by Lothian Health Board leading to separate dental practices in the town, all health services were integrated in these centres.

Although only intended as an interim measure until the new District Hospital opened, in practice the temporary status of the Howden health centre lasted for almost two decades. Plans for a new hospital in fact predated the designation of the new town. In 1957, the South East Regional Hospital Board decided to replace Bangour Hospital whose isolated location, poorly served by public transport, created problems for staff, patients and visitors alike.

As Bathgate could not provide a suitable site for the new hospital because of mining subsidence, the designation of Livingston solved a problem for the Health Board as well as providing a welcome boost for the new town. In 1964, a town centre location was agreed although five years later, when the design was changed from a high-rise block to the more spacious layout finally adopted, a larger 40 acre site in Howden West was chosen. In 1971, the green light was given for the first phase of the new hospital.

Planning a major hospital is much like planning a new town in miniature and a five year timescale was required. By 1973, the start to construction was put back to 1978, in part due to the reorganisation of the health service and the creation of Lothian Health Board. Continuing delays in commissioning the new hospital allowed support to grow for keeping it at Bangour, with Tam Dalyell an ardent campaigner. A start to building the hospital was eventually made in 1981.

The first phase of the hospital opened in 1990 creating 1,000 new jobs in the town. In line with its long held policy of providing housing for jobs, Howden finally got its permanent health centre within the hospital's precincts. With the opening of the second phase of St John's in 1991 by West Lothian NHS Trust, Livingston and West Lothian finally had a 600 bed hospital, whose consultant specialisms ranged from obstetrics to geriatrics.

A CHURCH FOR MANY FAITHS

As described more fully in a later chapter, Livingston's unique Ecumenical Experiment, with congregations from four different denominations sharing the same facilities, strongly influenced the building of Churches in the town. Each denomination took it in turn to fund the building of a church in a new district: the Church of Scotland in Craigshill, the Episcopal Church in Ladywell, the Congregationalists in Dedridge's Lanthorn.

Until appropriate buildings could be provided, residents worshipped in Riverside school. or travelled to an established Church in the vicinity. The

St John's
As well as providing a vital resource to the whole of West Lothian, St John's is a major town employer with a staff of 2,000. The people of Livingston are protective of their hospital and its environment. In 1995, they objected to a new incinerator converting hospital waste from East Central Scotland into energy being sited within the hospital precinct.

A Church Fit for an Experiment

The plain lines of St Columba's contrast with St Andrew's curves. Building St Columba's on a 1 in 10 slope meant using fixed pews, incompatible with the flexible space envisaged by the Ecumenical team. They protested to the architects in vain; then to the Presbytery, in vain. They appealed to the General Assembly, in vain. A year later, they appealed again. This time, the Assembly backed their plea and the Church was redesigned with a level floor and moveable seating.

foundation stone for St Columba's, Livingston's first new Church was laid in 1968 with a similar ceremony the next year for St Andrew's Roman Catholic Church, performed by Cardinal Gordon Gray, one of his first acts on elevation from Archbishop. The building of St Andrew's was held up by the bankruptcy of the contractor and it was not until 1970 that Cardinal Gray returned to bless the new Church.

Compared with much of the "no nonsense" architecture of the town and the stark simplicity of St Columba's, St Andrew's was a bold architectural gesture, with its concrete concentric curves winding up to a steep point. It was built to accommodate 450 people with standing room for a further 150.

Church building continued to address the needs of new districts and provide a permanent place of worship for smaller denominations such as the Free Church and the Baptists. St Columba's was augmented by St Paul's in Ladywell and in 1982, a second Roman Catholic church was opened at Carmondean, to serve the North end of the town. The South of the town was served by the last of the Ecumenical Churches housed within the Lanthorn Centre in Dedridge.

KRAZY KUTS OR SAFEWAYS

Livingston was served by mobile shops from neighbouring towns until its first shopping centre could be built. Housed in a temporary hut, the town's first new shop opened in April 1966, a newsagents and general store in Craigshill run by Billy Ritchie, the ex-Partick Thistle and Rangers goalkeeper.

Although its size was modest, Craigshill Shopping Mall claimed to be one of Scotland's first covered shopping centres. It consisted of a double lane of shops on the ground floor with small offices forming an upper floor on one side. The Shopping Mall catered largely for everyday purchases with tenants including the town's first banks, hairdresser, chemist and travel agent. The flagship was a Co-operative supermarket although many people continued to do their weekly shop in the Krazy Kuts, an early "deep discounter" in Pumpherston.

Initially, business was slow and in the first year, the traders won a 20% rent reduction because the customer base had not reached the predicted target. Maintenance was a continuing problem. It took a visit in 1969 by the Corporation's Chairman who complained about its untidy state and stained concrete to initiate action. A further clean-up including repainting the interior in vivid tones of white, orange and yellow was undertaken before the visit of the Secretary of State for Scotland, Willie Ross later in the same year.

In the 1970s, neighbourhood shopping centres were provided for almost all of the emerging districts. Because of its remoteness from the town centre, a larger centre was built at Carmondean with a Safeway's supermarket and smaller rettail units together with a health centre and library. As districts grew, convenience stores and newsagents moved in to the units provided by the Development Corporation. After, the opening of the first phase of the Almondvale Shopping Centre in 1977, Craigshill Shopping Mall lost its temporary "town centre" status. As part of the district's renewal, which lasted over a decade, part of the Mall was demolished being replaced by a free standing store and the rest remodelled in line with modern shopping trends.

EATING OUT AND DRINKING INN

Livingston's first purpose built pub and restaurant was the Tower in Craigshill. The inaugural pint was pulled by William Taylor, Chairman of the Development Corporation in November 1968 and a few weeks later, the Tower was advertising Christmas dinners at 21/- a head. In the early years, pubs both in the town and in the surrounding area helped to compensate for the lack of entertainment facilities, the bare-footed Sandie Shaw and Billy Connolly's Welly Boot Show being among the attractions.

For many years, Livingston had a direct influence on licensing proposals, operated through the Licensing Planning Committee. The aim was to provide a maximum of one off-licence, pub and social club for each district. It could prove difficult to reconcile the need to provide the town with facilities with the concerns of residents living near the chosen site. In 1972, for example, plans for Craigshill's second pub caused a furore because of its siting close to Craigshill High School. In 1980, the Secretary of State for Scotland decided to end this arrangement, leaving all licensing powers with the local authority Licensing Boards.

Livingston had to wait until 1985 for its first major hotel, the three star, 108 bedroom Livingston Ladbroke, now the Hilton, equipped with swimming pool, health club and training facilities for business. As the town's population reached 40,000, it became easier for the Corporation to attract commercial operators to provide amenities for eating out from

A Clean Place to Shop
When Craigshill Mall first opened, it was seen as the height of modernity and hygiene, compared with the old tenement shopping streets. Carmondean, with its supermarket, shops, health centre, library, garage, pub and takeaway shows how local shopping habits have changed again within the space of less than two decades.

The Beefeater Outside the Tower
The Tower was Livingston's first new public house. The town's first restaurant was a short lived venture in 1968 which soon changed into a shoe shop, despite a plea from local youngsters to turn it into a cafe. For the younger generation, the arrival of MacDonalds has marked Livingston's coming of age and for all generations, the Beefeater provides a place to do business over lunch or for a night out.

the Country Club attached to Deer Park Golf Course to a drive-in MacDonalds, the measure for many young people that a town is truly on the map.

A LETTER FROM LIVINGSTON

Until 1965, when Livingston became an address in its own right Livingston's postal address was Bathgate. The town's first sub-post office operated from a house in Craigshill, moving into the Shopping Mall in 1968. Three years later, a permanent sorting office to serve the town was opened in Cousland Road, with additional sub-post offices in the district shopping centres. Livingston finally won its own postal frank in 1973. Fears that the closure of the post office in the Almondvale Shopping Centre in 1994 and the transfer of transactions to ASDA, would lead to a reduction in services have so far proved groundless.

PARKS AND OPEN SPACES

Because of the difficulties of dealing with five District Councils whose finances were very limited and priorities different, the provision of district parks and sports grounds proved extremely problematic in the early years. The Corporation did what it could to provide funding to hasten the process but its own powers in this area were very limited.

Letham Park and Craigs Park, both in Craigshill, finally opened in the mid 1970s, after years of delays and wrangling. An additional delay was built in: even when sports areas were completed, at least one season had to elapse to allow the turf to grow. These parks provided badly needed sports pitches for tennis, bowls and football, as well as changing rooms and practice walls.

Local government reorganisation did not initially improve matters greatly with continuing debate between the Corporation, impatient for action and the Regional and District Councils as to who was responsible for what. From 1980, with leisure and recreation firmly in the court of the District Council and the additional resources of the MSC Community Programmes, the situation improved.

Play area provision proved controversial almost from the outset. The differing approaches of the small District Councils were reflected in the variety of types and level of provision. In 1975, the newly elected West Lothian District Council insisted that the provision of play areas was a housing matter, forcing the Corporation with some reluctance to take over responsibility for their construction and management. Carmondean won Playground of the Year Award from the National Playing Fields of

Scotland Association in 1978.

In private housing areas, play facilities provided by the developers to meet planning requirements increasingly gave rise to protests from adjoining residents. Despite its attempts to site facilities at a greater distance from houses, the Corporation found itself caught between groups of residents demanding that play areas should be provided close to home and equally vociferous groups demanding that they should not.

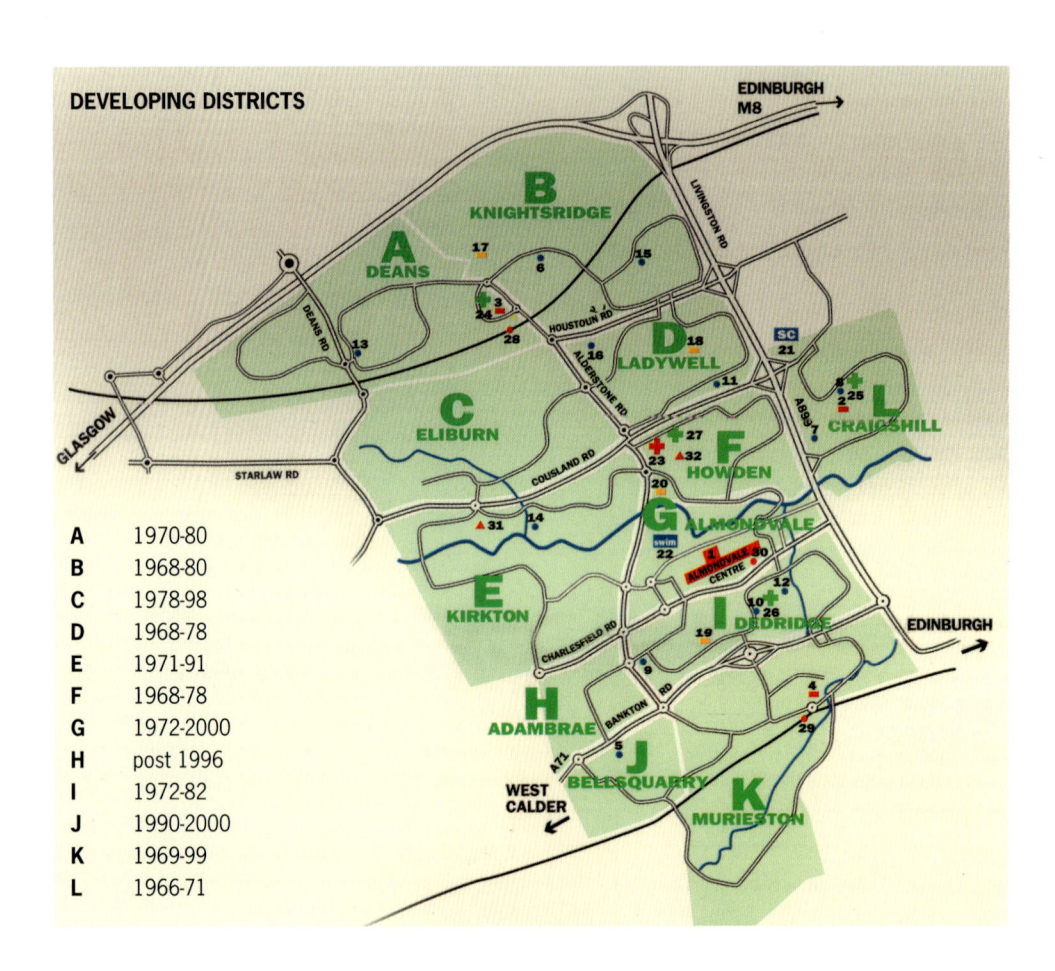

DEVELOPING DISTRICTS

A	1970-80
B	1968-80
C	1978-98
D	1968-78
E	1971-91
F	1968-78
G	1972-2000
H	post 1996
I	1972-82
J	1990-2000
K	1969-99
L	1966-71

·THE HEART AND LIFEBLOOD OF THE TOWN·

10
·BUILDING A COMMUNITY·

"In a true community, everybody feels either directly or through some group that he or she has a place and a part, belonging and counting. People cannot put down roots in nor feel responsibility for a place that does not give them that feeling." So, with great insight, wrote Lord Reith in 1946 in his Final Report of the New Towns Committee.

Over the next decade, in the rush to build new towns as quickly as possible, some of this spirit was lost. In 1959, the Carnegie United Kingdom Trust was joint sponsor of a two year study into "New Communities in Britain". The report reiterated that it was not enough for new towns to provide families with a house and a job and attributed most of their social problems to the process of adjustment.

Although its formal powers were limited, from the outset, Livingston Development Corporation was committed to helping its residents to adjust to their new life. It appointed Leslie Higgs as Scotland's first Social Relations Officer in 1963, combining the post with that of Housing Manager. Although a community can only be created by the people within it, the Corporation identified its role as facilitator in providing the appropriate support. This could be as simple as putting new residents in touch with others with similar interests or providing secretarial services for the reams of minutes and agendas on subjects as varied as campaigns for better bus services to organising the Livingston Festival. The mountain of paper grew higher and higher as the town developed.

SETTLING IN
The first priority in 1962 was to reassure the residents of Livingston Station about the major disruption to their lives. The second was to help the newcomers to settle in as quickly as possible, a difficult task when the population was still too small to justify resources. Aware of this Catch 22, many voluntary organisations led by the Churches were willing to take the gamble of putting in resources in advance of the population.

The task of the Corporation's housing staff and of many volunteers was to break the ice, by knocking on doors. In 1969, the town's ministers decided to visit every household. In their professional capacity, district nurses and midwives were in an unusually strong position to gain the confidence of young mothers. In many cases, they dedicated their spare time to setting up women's clubs and mother and toddler groups. These were completely informal networks, meeting in someone's house or a neighbourhood flat until the need for them was over.

THE PIONEERS
In the early years, the community spirit was strong. The town was so small that it was easy to at least recognise faces. Many of the first residents had made the very positive and deliberate choice, to create a new life in a pioneering community. This community spirit showed itself in very different ways. Despite freezing conditions, the 1968 bonfire night at Craigshill attracted a crowd of 500. The hot dog stall did a roaring trade with the profits going to Craigs Farm. A month later, the proposal by a few employees in Craigshill Mall for a Christmas night out at the Tower soon extended to a general invitation to all shop assistants in Livingston to join in.

In times of crisis, Livingston showed its community spirit. When an epidemic of Mao flu threatened in January, 1969, youth workers and doctors organised a flying squad of young people based at the Riverside Youth Wing to deliver prescriptions and check on households where both parents had been struck down by the bug. During the power cuts of the Three Day Week, residents were issued by the Corporation with a large "E" or "G" to display in their windows. People with gas could then help their less fortunate neighbours who had drawn the short straw of "E" for electricity.

THE ECUMENICAL EXPERIMENT
Much of the early success in creating a strong community can be attributed to the unique experiment in its midst, from which was to flow Craigs Farm, Forum and many other community initiatives. The early 1960s was a time of rapprochement among the world's faiths. In 1963, a conference of clerics in St Andrews sowed the seeds for the Ecumenical Experiment when they discussed new ways of expressing Church unity. The new

The Kindly Light
The building of the Lanthorn was the crowning point of the Ecumenical experiment. People like Ross McLaren, the Congregational minister, Father Byrne and Denis Barns, the Town Artist helped the new community to express its aspirations.

community of Livingston offered the opportunity to explore new ideas.

The Rev David Torrance, the Church of Scotland Minister of the joint charge of the Old Kirk of Livingston and St Andrews, Livingston Station took the idea forward which was finally adopted by the General Assembly in 1965 in designating Livingston as an area of Ecumenical Experiment. A Committee was set up representing the Church of Scotland, the Episcopal Church, the Congregational Church, the Methodists, the Baptists and the Salvation Army to oversee the experiment.

Church history was made on January 6th, 1966 when the Rev James Maitland of the Church of Scotland and the Rev Brian Hardy of the Scottish Episcopal Church were jointly inducted to their charge in a shared service at the Kirk of Calder. New ground was broken again on May 8th 1966 when the first service of the Ecumenical Experiment was held in Riverside Primary School. At a time when the town still had very few residents, the first congregation was small. About forty people met for coffee and an informal welcome before the actual service took place.

The bold concept behind the experiment was that instead of each church having its "parish", they would share pastoral duties, buildings and resources. The three founder Churches in the Experiment were the Church of Scotland, the Congregational Church and the Episcopal Church, with the Methodists joining in 1968.

An approach was made by Brian Hardy and James Maitland to the then Archbishop Gray to explore the extent to which the Roman Catholic Church might participate in the experiment and specifically to invite him to make an early appointment of a parish priest for Craigshill. Although doctrinal differences did not allow for full integration, the Cardinal did everything in his power to share in the spirit of the experiment by giving Father John Byrne, the town's first parish priest the freedom to conduct parish affairs as he saw fit. In 1971, the Cardinal invited the Servite order of nuns, founded in 13th century Florence, to set up a house in the town, where the support of a teacher, a social worker and a nurse was given to the Team Ministry.

Like the other individuals appointed by the Churches for their community leadership as well as spiritual qualities, Father Byrne was an inspired choice. He became a close friend of his colleagues within the Experiment, admired for his compassionate humanity and relied on for his wicked sense of humour. Churchgoers regularly found themselves attending the wrong service in the chaotic first days at Riverside School. The experiment reached its climax in the Lanthorn, where the Catholics although worshipping in a separate side chapel, shared a Communion table with the other joint congregation.

Not everyone could relate to this radical approach. Some residents who had been active participants in Church life in their previous homes preferred to attend the more traditional services held in the Old Kirk or in neighbouring towns, feeling the need for a symbol of stability in a sea of change. Others who previously had not been Church goers were drawn into the Church through the Experiment's informal approach and its active involvement in community affairs. Because of a different doctrinal approach, some denominations such as the Baptists felt unable to join the Experiment, although they contributed to a developing community in other ways. The sixty or so original members of the Baptist community met in people's homes, then Howden House until they could fund a new church of their own in Ladywell.

The Ecumenical Experiment formally ended in 1984 with the creation of Livingston Ecumenical Parish. The idea of moulding the Church into the life of the community continued with Dechmont Farm where the Church forms part of the Community Centre. The team approach is now a permanent fixture in Livingston parish.

FORUM

From those first, informal discussions over coffee before Church arose another of Livingston's unique institutions, Forum, the collective voice of the earliest residents. At first, the topics of conversation ranged from how to work the unfamiliar central heating to people's hopes for the town. These meetings increasingly attracted people whose primary interest was in the town rather than the Church service to the point where the actual congregation used to slip away in the midst of the discussion.

From simply a way of getting to know the neighbours, Forum quickly moved into a campaigning organisation to get things done. Thus it ensured that when Craigshill High opened, it had a headmaster, despite Midlothian County Council's proposal that the school could be served on a part-time basis by the head of West Calder High School. When problems emerged with the Jespersen flats, it was Forum which initiated the "Leaking Flats Committee" with Rev James Maitland as its chairman.

Forum's debates as to what was needed for the

What is a Community?

"The social process by which a community identifies its needs and objectives is one of continuous change." **Ron Aldous, Livingston's first Social Development Officer**

"The heart of the town is its people and this heart should beat loud and clear and not become blocked with a thrombosis of grumbles and discontent." **Lesley Higgs, Housing and Social Relations Manager**

"Like Topsy, the idea of a caring community just grows and grows." **Heather Birrell, new town resident and community leader**

"The aim of Community Development was to strike a balance between helping the community to articulate its needs and the Corporation's ability to meet them." **Graham Robertson, Head of Community Development, Livingston Development Corporation**

"One can do after three years what would have been quite unthinkable after one and after seven what could only be dreamt of after three." **Rev James Maitland**

New Uses for Old Farms

Although Craigs Farm was only rescued from the bulldozers by Forum's campaigners, the Corporation's later policy was to preserve old farmsteads unless beyond repair or directly in the path of development. Craigs Farm was the model for the later farm community centres - Nether Dechmont in Knightsridge, Crofthead in Dedridge and Newyearfield in Ladywell - often restored by Corporation managed MSC programmes:. Other farms have been put to different uses: Brucefield Farm as a bar and restaurant, Alderstone Mains as a garden centre, Bloom Farm as craft workshops with the adjacent farmhouse now housing the UK's first centre for people with epilepsy.

town led to some remarkable initiatives developed and run by volunteers. They included the first of many adventure playgrounds, held in the Easter holidays of 1969 with much of the equipment being donated by local manufacturers. Newsflash, the "self-propelled noticeboard" for the 1,400 households of Craigshill was launched by the team ministry in 1967 and then handed over to Forum where volunteers handled editorial and advertising. The same pattern of ministers and then Forum lay behind the establishment of Craigs Farm.

CRAIGS FARM & GRAIGSHILL INITIATIVE

Craigs Farm was the first and perhaps most enduring example of what local self-help could do, when a group of Craigshill residents pledged to create a youth and community centre out of the recently vacated farm buildings in their midst. Their first task was to save the building from the bulldozers. Although increasingly sympathetic to the importance of the old farms within the new community, the Corporation's immediate priority in Craigshill was to get houses built.

Volunteers carried out the conversion of the farm building while others applied their ingenuity to fundraising. Many ideas were tried including a rag collection and saving coppers. When it opened in the summer of 1969, Craigs Farm was described as "a service station for all sectors of the community."

Plans for opening up the West wing were launched in 1972. As well as an expansion of the highly successful nearly new shop, there was to be a cinema and theatre, built partly with the aim of demonstrating to commercial operators that there was a market for such facilities in the new town.

By the 1980s, under the dedicated management of John Hoey, Craigs Farm included a cafe, a print workshop, a craft shop and a toy library as well as continuing its fundamental role of providing a meeting space for local groups and a place where people could simply drop in for a chat. It was the one place where even Punks were welcome. Largely through the Corporation's MSC programmes, more of the outbuildings were converted for community use in the early 1980s, the first priority being a training workshop.

Through the Craigshill Initiative, the Corporation's Community Development team helped Craigshill residents to move towards a greater degree of self-empowerment. Out of endless and often heated discussions about the future of the community and its district came some creative proposals, including the establishment of one of Scotland's more profitable community businesses.

ROOMS, FARMS AND COMMUNITY CENTRES

Craigs Farm provided a model for some of the town's later community centres by demonstrating the appropriateness of reusing old buildings to form the heart of new communities. Each succeeding farm community centre had its own character and range of activities. The latest, Newyearfield farm, combines a community centre with space for small business.

Not every district, however, had a farm steading to build on. The range of organisations which helped to fund and manage Livingston's first purpose built community centres demonstrated their faith in the town. The Salvation Army was a partner with the Corporation in the community centre built behind the row of shops in Kingsport Avenue, Howden. The Congregational Church joined the local authorities and the Development Corporation in building the Lanthorn in Dedridge.

The aim of the Lanthorn was to "entertain, educate, inform and worship.". The complex containing community facilities, a branch library and a Church was planned in advance of the community moving in. Because Glaswegians were to make up a large part of the resident population, the steering group invited guests from the city to join them in their discussions as to the centre's role. These debates must have been heated on occasion given the comment in one report that "Glasgow people were wide open to criticism from other sections of the community for their own peculiar mannerisms. Care would have to be taken that this complex did not appear to be above their heads"

The Lanthorn marked the change towards a greater emphasis on the whole family in the design of community centres. A small community centre in Knightsridge grew into the multi-purpose Mosswood Centre, a partnership between the Development Corporation and Lothian Regional Council. As well as community meeting space, the Harrysmuir Community Pavilion, opened in 1971 by Lord Linlithgow, included tennis courts, a bowling green, a paddling pool and a children's play area.

The role of community centres changed with the needs of the local residents as each district matured. By the end of the 1970s, the Corporation was helping to provide everything from play group huts, to community houses, neighbourhood flats and meeting rooms, in addition to its participation in the major community centres for the town. It made available accommodation to local groups and associations, often at the peppercorn rent of £1 a year.

The development of community centres was as

No Home to Call One's Own

Livingston Action on Teenage Homelessness was formed. by the community in response to one of the inevitable problems of a young town. In 1984, the Corporation reduced the minimum age for tenancies to 17 and created a new letting priority for people with "urgent social needs." Working with Open Door, in 1985, the Corporation identified the need for emergency accommodation and counselling for homeless teenagers.

The support of Lothian Regional Council, West Lothian District Council and the Aberlour Childcare Trust was enlisted, with the Corporation offering six flats in Craigshill for emergency accommodation and six flats throughout the town as supported accommodation. It actively sought the partnership of other agencies such as specialist housing associations, although efforts could on occasion be thwarted by the reaction of local residents who did not want "problem teenagers" as next door neighbours.

A New Challenge
A sense of community extended to the next generation. In Britain's youngest town, it was a constant battle to keep up with demand for facilities like creches and play schemes, although the Corporation's policy of providing play areas meant that there was always a log to climb or a chance of "a shot on the swings".

varied as the districts of the town. Knightsridge illustrates the overall pattern. In 1978, a community house was opened to welcome families to the district. By 1982, this had progressed to providing accommodation for the Citizens Advice Bureau, the Scottish Council on Alcoholism and a mother and baby clinic. In the early 1980s, the Save the Children Fund became involved in assisting to meet the needs of a very young population with a higher than average proportion of single parents, with Princess Anne, its patron, opening the adventure playground which evolved from its family centre in 1983.

THE UK'S YOUNGEST TOWN
Catering for ever growing numbers of young people was one of the first challenges faced by the Development Corporation and its partners. In January, 1965, 26 representatives of 15 organisations with an involvement in youth, from the Scottish Association of Young Farmers' Clubs to the Council of Churches, met to discuss the issue, forming the Provision for Youth committee which met regularly to review the position.

At the end of 1966, they decided that Craigshill was sufficiently far advanced to merit its own sub-committee of new town residents. Meeting for over a decade, this sub-committee was influential in persuading many youth organisations such as the Brownies and the Boys Brigade to set up in the town.

In 1965, Max Cruickshank, the town's first youth worker, funded by the Church of Scotland, was appointed, with the somewhat cumbersome title of Youth Adviser to the Livingston and Bathgate Presbytery. He operated largely out of the Youth Wing, attached to Riverside Primary School. which included a dance area, a coffee bar, a games room, work room and dark room for photography. In 1966, he was joined by Ron Aldous, the Corporation's first Community Development Officer, whose remit was town-wide: to bring residents together, to seek out community leaders and to assist local people to contribute actively to the life of the town.

Providing facilities for young people was primarily the responsibility of the Education Department of the two County Councils. Their policies differed markedly with Midlothian building Youth Wings attached to local primary schools and West Lothian preferring self-contained community centres such as Knightsridge for both adults and young people.

Initially, the focus of the Youth Wings was to provide a space where teenagers could meet informally with no restrictions other than a ban on smoking. As the town grew up and the interests of young people changed from "hops" to "discos", from listening to records to playing computer games, the programmes of activities kept pace, organised largely by local volunteers under the supervision of a youth worker. As with all aspects of community life, the youth centres evolved over time to cater for different demands and to make best use of scarce resources. In the early 1980s, the Dedridge Youth Centre opened its doors not only to unemployed young people but to toddlers through a pre-school play group while the public could drop in for a coffee in the cafe.

Finding and training enough volunteers was a constant problem as was funding professional youth workers. Rejecting one of many applications for a youth worker in 1972, the Director of Education of Midlothian County Council wrote "Social workers in Livingston are finding that the immediate demands made on them by families who clamour for attention, prevent any selectivity of work to be usefully undertaken or for any overall project to be set up which could be seen as preventative rather than first aid."

There was also the issue of making contact with those young people to whom organised social activities did not appeal, especially when Livingston had virtually nowhere else for them to go. Livingston Community Council, the successor to Forum, was instrumental in raising funding from a number of Churches and other bodies to appoint the town's first detached youth worker in 1973. Young people in Livingston could have a hard time. By the late 1970s, jobs were not easy to come by, and as in any town, vandalism, under-age drinking, homelessness and drugs were constant concerns. In Livingston, the sheer number of young people made the problems more visible.

AND THE NOT SO YOUNG

As the town developed, the Corporation had to focus its attention on the needs of many different parts of the community, women, the elderly and the disabled among them. The Corporation's role was primarily as instigator, of attracting the appropriate voluntary and caring bodies to the town and helping them to find their feet. Livingston grew up alongside the increasing national trend for women to work. The new industries which the town was attracting especially electronics and office processing had a particularly high requirement for female workers. Going out to work also offered a solution to the need to stretch the family budget further in a new town.

After years of negotiation, Midlothian County Council finally agreed to staff the town's first day

Lunch Club to Day Centre

As early as 1971, there were nine organisations offering activities for older people from carpet bowls to cribbage. The early lunch clubs were run largely by volunteers, with the first dedicated centre established in Howden House by the Livingston Old People's Welfare Committee. In the late 1970s with Corporation support, Lothian Regional Council invested £500,000 in Braid House, Almondvale with a lunch club for the frail elderly as well as a drop-in centre for all senior citizens. In 1987, Braid House moved again to the refurbished former Howden Health Centre. The Chair of the Braid House Management Committee for many years was Mrs Audrey Wilson, the wife of the Corporation's third General Manager.

Read All About It

A sign that a new town has arrived is when it acquires its own newspaper. Thanks to the far sightedness of the local newspaper group, the Johnston Press of Falkirk, the first edition of the Livingston Post was published on Hallowe'en, 1968, at a time when the town only had a population of 7,000. The front page headline proclaimed "NEW TOWN NOW HAS ITS OWN NEWSPAPER alongside a photograph of Craigshill captioned "the trim, geometric lines of the houses married to the lush green of the surrounding landscape seems to epitomise the character of Scotland's modern cities." By 1971, the volume of news was sufficient to justify the move from tabloid to broadsheet although the price remained at 4d.

nursery which the Corporation had offered to build, in 1973. Almost twenty years later, the Corporation helped Careshare, to open the town's first private creche. In the intervening years, mothers campaigned for better provision, queued up for places in the small but gradually growing number of nurseries and creches or formed their own playgroups and holiday schemes.

Livingston Old People's Welfare Committee was established in 1969 with an inaugural lunch served by the local Brownies in Riverside School. Soon, it was running its first two lunch clubs in Howden and Craigshill for the town's 100 old age pensioners. By the early seventies, there were over sixty clubs and services specifically for old people from a mobile chiropodist to bingo nights. Over the next two decades, demand increased as the town's population grew older to the point where now several organisations run reminiscence groups where older people relive their first days as new town pioneers.

INFORMING THE COMMUNITY

Along with countless volunteers and voluntary bodies, Livingston Development Corporation played its part in the essential role of telling people what was going on in the town and in ensuring that communication networks were fostered. In most housing districts, the Corporation set up a mobile caravan as soon as the first families moved in. Because of its initial isolation from the rest of the town, however, Knightsridge like Craigshill had a permanent office right from the start which dealt with all enquiries and problems other than the payment of rents.

In 1973, to supplement Newsflash, the Corporation produced, "What's On in Livingston", giving details of community, arts and sporting events in the town. The publication continued to be produced on a quarterly then two monthly basis. Livingston Life was launched in 1976 to inform the growing community about the Corporation's involvement in the many facets of town life.

A very different information resource operated in the town centre from the mid 1970s. Instigated by Livingston Community Council and modelled on Communicare at Killingworth near Newcastle, the Community Resource Centre provided a space where all the town's many caring organisations could offer a one-door service, as well as offices for the Council of Churches, the Citizens Advice Bureau, the Livingston Voluntary Organisations Council and some of the Corporation's own housing and community development staff. The Corporation provided accommodation, initially in temporary premises in Braid House and then in Lammermuir House, with the former becoming an old people's day centre.

A VOICE FOR THE TOWN

At an Edinburgh University conference on the social implications of New Towns in 1968, the Rev Hamish Smith identified the key needs of the community as being representation and participation. "If residents are not allowed to participate in the creation of community life then New Towns will become concentration camps at the worst or dormitory camps at the best. The basic concept of community life is personal not physical and there is a limit to planned planning."

Two factors spurred the evolution of Forum into Scotland's first Community Council. By 1970, numbers attending Forum were dropping and as people moved into other districts, there was increasing debate as to whether Forum should be the voice of Craigshill or of the town as a whole. The concept of Community Councils was emerging in the discussions over local government reform as a way of retaining community involvement after the removal of the bottom tier of elected government.

Such a Council could be a possible mechanism to keep open the invaluable line of communication between groups of local residents and statutory bodies responsible for community services. Innovative to the last, Forum itself took on the task of shaping its successor body. In 1971, it set up a Community Research Group which after a year of consultation and studying experience elsewhere presented its proposals to a series of public meetings throughout the town. With a formal constitution, the Council consisted of up to four members elected from each of the six housing districts. Its objectives were to seek out and represent community opinion, to act as a link between the people and the public authorities and to co-ordinate the activities of voluntary organisations in the town.

The Community Council for Livingston, to give it its formal title, held its first meeting in the Corporation's offices, with John Ross, the headmaster of Riverside Primary as its Chairman. As a new organisation with few parallels to draw on, the Community Council had to feel its way by trial and error. The first meetings in 1972 raised issues which were to remain on the agenda of the Council and its successor organisations for many years: the inadequacy of bus services, the lack of activities for young people, overcrowding in primary schools, the problem of roaming dogs. The Council campaigned, cajoled and complained, winning the respect of the Development Corporation and the other bodies with which it dealt.

From 1975, Community Councils were established throughout Scotland as part of local government reform. Rather than keeping with their unique arrangement, Livingston decided to follow the national pattern with Councils being set up in eight districts of the town. Like Community Councils

A Royal Playground

The Corporation used its Major Amenity Fund to build the Knightsridge Family Centre alongside the existing community Pavilion. As patron of the Save the Children Fund, Princess Anne had a close association with the charity's work in Knightsridge, opening the Family Centre in 1981 and visiting its Adventure Playground in 1983. Knigthsridge Adventure Playground was the first Scottish new town project to be awarded Urban Aid funding.

everywhere, recruiting members proved a continuing struggle but meetings were well attended whenever an issue arose to threaten the interests of the district or town. Some Community Councils, notably Bellsquarry, Dedridge and Knightsridge have succeeded in maintaining an active involvement from residents for nearly twenty years.

LIVINGSTON VOLUNTARY ORGANISATIONS COUNCIL

From the Community Council for Livingston came Livingston Voluntary Organisations Council. One of the aims of the Community Council was to co-ordinate the activities of local voluntary bodies. To address this, from 1973, the Social Workers Lunch Club, a group of representatives from voluntary and statutory caring bodies, met informally in St Paul's Church in Ladywell. From one of their discussions emerged the idea to create a support agency for the fast multiplying number of voluntary, community and leisure groups in the town. With the support of the Corporation's Community Development staff, this idea was taken forward to become Livingston Voluntary Organisations Council in 1974, the same year that Livingston's first Community Directory was produced.

The Council set out to identify gaps in provision, bring people together, campaign, lobby and initiate. In the words of its first organiser, Heather Birrell, "essentially its business was about making the machinery work." The Council's activities over the next two decades are a history of the social and community life of the town and of issues faced across the country - homelessness, provision for the under fives, glue sniffing, child abuse, Care in the Community, even distributing the EEC butter and beef mountains and the proceeds of the BBC's Children in Need appeal.

It initiated or partnered many of Livingston's later community projects from the YWCA Neighbourhood Houses in Craigshill and Howden to the furniture recycling store at Craigs Farm and the placing of the Corporation's Community Programme volunteers with community groups. It set up a charitable fund to help disabled children whose scope was later widened to included disadvantaged children in the town. In 1993, the organisation was subsumed into the new Voluntary Action West Lothian.

11
THIRTY YEARS OF FUN AND GAMES

Bricks and mortar are one thing but it is what people do with them that matters. This was one of the lessons learned from the first generation of Britain's new towns, where the focus was very much on developing the physical environment occasionally at the expense of the spirit of the town.

As far as was possible within the limits of its remit from Government and also of its own budget and resources, the Corporation set out to foster the spirit of Livingston, especially in the early years when the town was still forming the network of organisations and enthusiasts who would carry the spirit forward.

MAKING OUR OWN ENTERTAINMENT

Residents from the cities were used to having entertainment on their doorstep whereas in Livingston, people were often initially forced back on their own resources. These turned out to be considerable, laying the foundations for the 400 organisations that thrive in the town today.

Some people already had hobbies and interests which they wanted to continue. Others simply wanted to meet people. In 1966, a group of men got together in Riverside School for a weekly games night, forming the nucleus of the Craigshill Social Club. They organised the building and running of the Club, attracting funding from a ten year deal with Scottish & Newcastle Breweries. Opening in 1969, the Craigshill Social Club aimed for a "country club atmosphere", with a hall for 500 people, a lounge, a games room and meeting rooms. The Club also promoted a range of activities from judo, darts and fishing to regular trips to other parts of the country. Its popularity permitted an extension a few years later. In the early 1980s, the residents of Dedridge came together to set up a similar social club for their area.

By the creative use of its Minor Amenities Fund, the Corporation could help groups who wished to set up a new club or interest. While many organisations like the Cubs and Brownies had their own established procedures, the challenge for the Corporation's staff was to find, introduce and support residents who enjoyed an interest such as chess and who might, therefore be interested in setting up a Club.

In 1980, the Corporation rented out six flats in Craigshill to a group of hobbyists who sought joint facilities to pursue aeromodelling, model railways, wildlife, photography, aquarium building and mountaineering.

Opening Up the Arts
By the time Andrew Cruickshank gave the Howden Park Centre a clean bill of health in 1972, community activity throughout the town included: the Almond Singers, amateur dramatics and operatics, archery, aeromodelling, art, badminton, basketball, billiards, bingo, boxing, bridge, carpet bowls, ceilidhs, chess, cine, concert parties, crafts, curling, dancing, darts, discos, dog training, fishing, floral art, football, golf, gymnastics, jazz, judo, mill restoration, model railways, outdoor bowls, pigeon homing, piping, politics, rugby, swimming, lawn and table tennis, trampolining, women's clubs, a youth band, youth clubs and much needed, free baby sitting circles.

Top of the Bill
A regular billing at the Mews Theatre was the review mounted by local resident, Beryl Beattie, who put her experience as a Five Past Eight Show dancer to good use.. To outsiders, Beryl is better known for her weekly advertising column in The Scotsman.

HOWDEN HOUSE TO HOWDEN CENTRE

In the early years of the Corporation's life, there was a continuing debate as to the extent to which it should actively encourage townspeople to promote cultural activities. Here, the Corporation's role was often as catalyst, providing the resources and expertise to get things started. In 1969, for example, staff wrote to a number of theatres including the Citizens and the Traverse to suggest that they might like to bring performances to the town.

Howden House was the town's first public building. In 1964, Livingston was fortunate in attracting support from the UK Carnegie Trust, whose founder, the multi-millionaire, Andrew Carnegie, had funded libraries and other public buildings throughout his home country. In the early 1960s, the Trust had voiced its concern that new towns had neglected the social and cultural needs of their citizens.

Prepared to back its concerns with cash, the Trust agreed to donate £12,000 towards the restoration of the 18th century Howden House for community use, on two conditions: that it was ready by the time that the first families moved in and that the Corporation contributed to its running costs until the local organisations using the Centre were sufficiently established to be able to afford the full rent.

On 23rd July, 1966, Howden House was opened by Baroness Elliott of Harwood, the Chairman of the Trust and widow of a former Secretary of State for Scotland. Managed by the Corporation, it provided meeting rooms for local groups provided they were "of lasting benefit to the town" and offices for organisations such as the Citizens Advice Bureau and the YWCA Howden House proved an enduring asset to the town. Within a few years of its opening, it was used on over 1,200 occasions. Its grounds became Livingston's first park for family outings as well as the venue for fetes and Festivals.

Fittingly, on his last day in office, Brigadier Purches announced plans for the creation of an arts centre based on the stable block of Howden House. It provided the Mews Theatre and accommodation for groups involved in the arts. Although originally planned as a joint venture between the Corporation, the Livingston Arts Association and the Livingston Players, the Corporation ended up financing the whole project as the hoped for sponsorship did not materialise. The Livingston Operatic Society put on South Pacific to mark the opening and the start of the town's tenth birthday celebrations. The Scottish actor Andrew Cruickshank, best known for his role as the senior partner in Dr Finlay's Casebook, performed the opening ceremony.

The Corporation converted some of the outbuildings for a conference and meeting centre, the revenue from which helped to maintain the upkeep of the complex as well as providing a suitable venue for the Corporation itself to entertain VIPs and foreign visitors. In its first year, it hosted 24 conferences and commercial events, as well as welcoming visitors from 20 countries.

A further dimension to Livingston's cultural life was added in 1987 when the Corporation helped the West Lothian Youth Theatre to establish a base in Craigs Park, the first youth theatre in the UK to have a permanent home.

FESTIVALS AND BIRTHDAYS

With their parades through the streets and children's sports, Gala days were a long standing tradition in the mining communities of West Lothian. In the early years of the new town, Livingston Station and Village continued to hold their annual events. Livingston's tenth birthday celebrations in 1972 provided the impetus for the new town to provide its own unique contribution to this tradition.

The birthday was marked by a week of celebrations. Like the Olympics, they started with the pupils of Craigshill High descending on Howden Park from all corners of the town to light an anniversary flame. This was accompanied by the release of pigeons and balloons, one of which was found 400 miles away. The Scotland England match at Hampden competed with or perhaps was the reason behind a Ladies Football match on the opening afternoon. Events during the week-long celebration included art and industrial exhibitions, the Livingston Village Gala and schools open days. The Festival ended with fireworks and a jazz concert.

At the end of the anniversary week, the Chairman of Livingston Development Corporation issued the challenge that it should become an annual event. Perhaps because of the hiatus between Forum and Community Council, at first it looked as if nothing would happen. In the last weeks of 1972, with the support of the Corporation, the Community Council agreed that they would take on the role of Festival organisers, provided the community was prepared to participate. Several groups, notably the Howden Ladies Social Club rose to the occasion and extremely tight timescales and poor weather failed to dampen the success of the first of what became an annual event in Livingston's calendar.

In many ways, the 1973 Festival set the pattern for the years to come. The week opened with a parade of floats from each housing district and

Shake It All About
Tam Dalyell, the local MP, revealed an unexpected talent for nimble footwork at the opening of an early Livingston Festival. In 1983, the town gained its own constituency and MP, Robin Cook, now Shadow Foreign Secretary.

The Royal Diary

1967 The Duke of Edinburgh opens Cameron Iron Works • 1970 Princess Anne visits the Almondell Project • 1971 The Duke of Edinburgh visits MOTEC • 1976 The Duke of Edinburgh attends a Scottish Design Council conference on "Success from Innovation." • 1978 The Queen goes walkabout. • 1981 Princess Anne opens the Save the Children Fund Family Centre • 1981 The Duke of Kent performs the opening ceremony of the National Electronics Council's symposium. • 1983 The Queen opens the NEC semiconductor plant • 1983 Princess Anne visits the Knightsridge Adventure Playground. • 1987 The Queen celebrates Livingston's Silver Jubilee • 1989 Prince Charles hosts the first Prince's Trust Conference. • 1990 The Queen opens the first phase of St John's Hospital • 1994 The Queen opens the Bloom House children's centre.

ended with a fireworks display in Howden Park. Schools and housing districts competed against each other at everything from football to It's a Knockout, based on the popular TV series. There was an art exhibition, schools open days and a motor gymkhana within the grounds of MOTEC.

Local communities within the town also developed their own gala days and in time these caused a conflict of priorities with the town wide Festival. There simply were not enough volunteers and sponsors to go round. The Festival retreated into a one day event. With the creation of the Town Forum in 1995, there are plans to revive the town wide Festival tradition.

Another addition to the calendar of events in which Livingston Community Council played a major role was the annual Garden Competition from September, 1973. Building on the success of the Livingston Station Garden and Allotments Association and a competition for the town sponsored by the Corporation the previous year, the two initiatives were merged in the Livingston Garden Association. Livingston gardeners had some unusual problems to contend with in mud, builder's rubble and topsoil which had barely time to settle. Recognising this, the Corporation donated a special prize for the products of a "virgin garden", one which had been established for less than a year, and a conifer to all prize winners to mark "Plant a Tree in 73".

Festivals were also organised to mark special occasions, initiated by the Corporation's Community Development team and the Livingston Voluntary Organisations Council. In 1975, they jointly organised an exhibition in Howden Park to celebrate UN International Women's Year and in 1979, mounted the Young Livingston exhibition and "the Child and the Family" seminar to mark the International Year of the Child. In 1981, a similar event was hosted for the International Year for Disabled People.

1987 was a Jubilee rather than just a birthday. The town was honoured by a visit from the Queen to help it celebrate its silver jubilee. The first of many Children's Carnivals was held in the Forum as part of the celebrations and every young person in the town was presented with a copy of William Hendrie's History of Livingston as a memento. The next year, it was Glasgow's turn to celebrate, with Livingston hosting a Tram Stop at the Garden Festival.

A feature of many Festivals in Scotland is participation by performers from the town's overseas "twin". Unlike the other Scottish New Towns, Livingston never established a formal town twinning arrangement. The Corporation decided instead to provide financial support to the West Lothian Town Twinning Association, under whose auspices many of the town's young people went on exchange visits to Hochsauerlandkreis in Germany.

SLIGHTLY OUT OF FOCUS

A night at the pictures was an early priority for the town despite the fact that in the 1960s and 1970s cinema going was in steep decline. Although their original purpose had been to bring the cinema to remote, rural communities, the Highlands and Islands Film Guild already had new town experience, putting on shows in Cumbernauld and Glenrothes, before being approached by Livingston Development Corporation.

The Guild agreed to put on a Tuesday night film show for adults and a Saturday children's matinee in the Deans Institute, the only venue large enough to take the projection equipment. The big picture on the first night at the end of November 1968 was the thriller "Jack of Diamonds." Sadly, the experiment only lasted four months. Dwindling audiences with as few as twelve devotees and the difficulty of moving the heavy projection equipment led to the decision to abandon the adult screenings, although weekly film shows for children continued at the Riverside Youth Wing for some time. thereafter.

In 1972, another attempt was made to put Livingston on screen. Charles Williams, a Livingston resident and one of Scotland's top projectionists, founded a Film Society with free membership to OAPs. The opening night in the Mews Theatre was inauspicious: after an hour, "Paint Your Wagon" had to be abandoned when the sound track broke down and the picture stubbornly remained out of focus. The club folded not long after.

The town is still waiting for its own cinema. As part of the first phase of the Almondvale Shopping Centre, a commercial cinema was opened by Caledonian Associated Cinemas but after several years of operation, it was converted to a bingo hall, owing to lack of demand. With vastly increased audiences in the 1990s, the provision of a cinema is back on the agenda with proposals for a major leisure complex.

FOOTBALL V VOLLEYBALL

The story of sport in Livingston is a mix of the traditional and enduring activities of football and bowls and the successive "crazes" which were popular especially among young people from BMX to roller blading. In the 1970s the passion was for volleyball inspired by the Olympics whereas in the 1980s

Prime Time
Beechgrove Garden was not the only time that Livingston has been transmitted nationwide. It has hosted "Down Your Way" and "Any Questions", led "Songs of Praise" and acted as the model for a radio soap, "Killbreck", as well as been the subject of several schools and current affairs broadcasts.

On Cue
Steve and Joe Davis make a break in Livingston. Steve was later to take on Stephen Hendry in a contest of the gladiators at the Forum in 1988.

technology allowed skates to become skateboards.

Golf was an early priority for Livingston given that any self respecting Scottish town has its own course. There was the added impetus of the attraction of the game to US and Japanese businessmen. The Corporation originally developed the golf course at Deer Park in 1978 in partnership with Miller Buckley. When the agreement ended, the Corporation took the opportunity to market the golf course to other operators with the requirement that there should be a significant upgrading of facilities. A decade later, the Muir Group opened the Deer Park leisure complex, with, in addition to an 18 hole championship golf course, ten pin bowling, squash courts, snooker, a swimming pool and a solarium.

As well as the provision of facilities for specific outdoor sports, the Corporation recognised the need to provide freely available unsupervised activity areas. The first of the these projects was the Trim Course, in Almondvale Park, a gentle obstacle course for residents to keep fit or lose a few pounds. In the early 1980s, a unique "sports landscape" was developed alongside the Trim Course attracting finance from the Scottish Sports Council as an experiment in integrating the needs of a diverse range of recreational activities. The landscape included a climbing wall, an area for roller skating and a skateboard rink, claimed to be the largest in Europe.

THE LIVINGSTON LEISURE CALENDAR

It would take a book in itself to describe the activities of the town's societies and clubs, the achievements of individuals and teams, the big events and the regular features. This can only be a taster of the richness and diversity of the social, cultural, community and sporting life of a town which already has many memories.

1968   *Livingston Rugby Club played its first home game in a field leased to it by the Corporation along with two farm cottages at Bankton for changing rooms.*

1969   *Livingston was the first new town to commission a film of its progress. "The Seven Springs of Livingston", later titled "A Place for Living" made by the Films of Scotland Committee and launched at the Edinburgh Festival documented the first seven springs of the town's life.*

1970   *New community organisations started up with interests as varied as boxing and Highland dancing, bringing the total to over 60.*

1971   *The first attempt to hold a Civic Week foundered when only six people turned up at a public meeting to recruit volunteers.*

1972   *The Corporation appointed a full time Play Officer to organise summer play schemes.*

1973   *The Livingston Youth Trust funded places for eight boys on the adventure schooner, Captain Scott.*

1974   *Livingston's first Community Directory helped residents to find out what was happening and who was organising it.*

1975   *The Livingston Lectures, a series on topics of importance to the Scottish economy were launched.*

1976   *There were now 230 community organisations, one for every 100 people.*

1977   *The Livingston Crafts Association held its first craft fair with 2,000 visitors and 35 stalls.*

1978   *The first golfer tee-ed off at the Deer Park course.*

1979   *The Corporation repositioned boulders in the Almond to allow canoe runs without disturbing the traditional pursuits of anglers.*

1980   *Livingston offered the widest range of activities in Scotland associated with the annual Sport for All Week.*

1981   *The Livingston Festival became the largest community Festival in Scotland.*

1982   *Livingston's Rock 'n' Roll Skatepark was the venue for a display from two of the world's best skateboarders from the USA.*

1983   *The Livingston International Sports Trust was launched to help gifted individuals achieve their potential.*

1984   *The Livingston Charities Fayre was visited by a flying Santa Claus.*

1985   *Livingston hosted the first Scottish Youth Theatre's Summer Festival, while Livingston Brass Band achieved Champion status.*

1986   *Crofthead Community Farm opened providing toddlers with a new adventure and older people with a cup of tea and a chat.*

1987   *Over 1,500 runners took part in the Livingston half marathon.*

1988   *The Scottish under 25s Professional Golf Championship, sponsored by the Corporation, was won by local golfer, Gordon Law.*

1989   *No fewer than five official effigies of Guy Fawkes topped the town's bonfires.*

1990   *Runrig, Scotland's top band, played at the Forum.*

1991   *The Livingston Kings ice hockey and the Livingston Bulls basketball teams finished the season at the top of their respective leagues.*

1992   *Livingston made the Top Twenty with David Cicero's "Love is Everywhere"*

1993   *Livingston hosted the European Model Stock Car championships on its new racing oval, and Olympic ice dancers performed at the international Ice Gala.*

1994   *Kids had adventures in the unique shale oil playground at the Almond Valley Heritage Centre.*

1995   *The meteoric rise of Livingston FC in its first season looks set to continue Like the town, according to the sports press "Livingston is going from strength to strength".*

1996   *Livingston's first, dedicated cricket ground was completed.*

Bridging the Almond
The 18th century stone arches of the bridge in Livingston Village contrast with the 10 span award winning Almond Valley Bridge. The Almond now has nine new bridges for vehicles and pedestrians.

12
·FITTING THE PIECES TOGETHER·

INFRA-WHAT?

Like all professionals, planners, engineers and administrators have their own jargon. One term they share is "infrastructure". To the rest of us, this simply means all the roads, footpaths, sewers and utilities like gas and electricity which tie a town together and make it function. We happily take these for granted except when they are not there. Although we think of woodlands and open spaces in terms of what they add to our surroundings, they too are part of this infrastructure in that they help to draw individual buildings together to make the coherent whole which we think of as a town.

In a new town like Livingston where nothing existed on the ground already, putting in the infrastructure involved a huge investment by the Corporation, the local authorities and the utility providers as well as presenting an enormous challenge for those responsible for its design and co-ordination. The planning and programming of Livingston's infrastructure had a major bearing on the shape of the town and how it evolved.

Building the town in strips from east to west was not simply to give it a coherent identity. This progression was also dictated by the common sense of using roads, drains and all the other services as efficiently as possible. Because the main sewage treatment plant had to be built adjacent to the river downstream from the town, it was economic to start building in Craigshill which was closest to this point, thereafter moving westwards and outwards

By and large, the same discipline applied to most aspects of development, even landscaping. As far as finance permitted, trees were planted well in advance of house or factory building. None the less, planting followed the same east to west pattern. It was, therefore, as late as March, 1996 before the western extremity of the Almond, virtually the last section of the town's linear parkway, was landscaped.

PAST LEGACY

The first task was to remove the depredations of previous generations. Conscious of its role in setting the highest environmental standards, the Corporation arranged to remove or landscape virtually all of the derelict features within the designated area. The most dramatic change came with the disappearance of the Deans Bing which once overshadowed Livingston Station. Over the years, more than a billion cubic metres of blaise were removed from bings such as Deans which were not only used in the construction of town roads including Houstoun Road and Cousland Road and also sold to contractors building the M8 and the M74. In 1983, the by now much diminished bing was shaped and landscaped to form Deans South West Industrial Estate.

An unexpected challenge arose in 1994 when it was discovered that ash underlying topsoil in part of the Murieston Valley area would need to be removed to make the land suitable for housing. After much discussion with local residents, a major engineering operation was successfully completed by the end of 1995.

FIRST THINGS FIRST

An immediate priority was to ensure that the new town had the essential services of water, sewerage and communications. Over the succeeding decades, the first sign of a new industrial or residential district was when the engineers moved in.

Adequate water supplies presented only a short term problem. In 1962, Livingston was served by the small Dechmont reservoir but the opening of the West Water reservoir in the Pentland Hills in 1965 provided the town with 3m gallons a day, more than ample to meet its early needs. From 1967, half the town drew its supplies from Loch Lomond, although this turned out to be not without its problems. The original brass plumbing fittings installed in the first housing districts had to be replaced when the exceptionally soft water started to dissolve the zinc in the pipes. In later years, most of the town's water came from the much enhanced reservoir system within the Lothians.

It was clear from the start that the existing sewerage system would be unable to cope with a new town. Midlothian County Council opened the first phase of a new sewage and waste water treatment plant at East Calder in 1968 with further phases opening as the town grew. For many years, it looked as if this plant could meet the town's needs for the foreseeable future.

Two very different demands were to alter this position: the sheer volume of water processed by several of the town's high technology industries and new European environmental legislation. In 1995, East of Scotland Water and the Corporation jointly funded a £5m water treatment plant at Kirkton, to

Bigger is Better
Putting in essentials like drainage and sewerage was the first sign that a new district was opening up. In order to inspire investor confidence in the future growth of the town, the Corporation and its partners endeavoured to provide utilities with a much greater capacity than immediately required as here at East Calder Sewage Plant.

***River Crossings**
Just as in previous centuries, first the canal then the railway had to be carried over the Almond Valley, in the early 70's, it was to be crossed again by the M8 and by Livingston Road.*

ensure that the town could accommodate further high technology industry until such time, expected to be around 1998, as the River Almond Purification Scheme could be implemented.

Supplying the new town with electricity and gas presented few difficulties with gas initially coming from the revolutionary Lurgi coal gasification plant in Fife. In the early 1970s, Livingston like everywhere else was subjected to the disruption of conversion to North Sea gas.

The first telephone equipment was housed in two caravans until a permanent exchange to the south of Ladywell was opened in 1969. From the start, the GPO was committed to providing the new town with the most advanced telephone services. Although there were only 400 telephone lines in Livingston when the Exchange opened, it could handle 3,000 with the potential to expand to 8,000 as the town grew. Later that year, local numbers were extended from 4 to 5 digits to allow for the introduction of STD and direct dialling. In 1972, the GPO sited its telephone engineering depot for West Lothian in the town.

Livingston had an early form of cable TV. In 1965, the Board decided to invite British Relay to provide the town with television through underground cables to avoid the clutter of roof top aerials which marred the skyline of most towns. This decision was less popular with residents who regularly complained about the quality of their picture, the extra cost of renting a special set, and the speed of repairs.

By the mid 1970s, the Corporation decided to end the system which in any case had not been extended to some of the outlying districts and to private housing estates. Instead, the Corporation brought in regulations to ensure that the siting of aerials and later, of satellite dishes, involved the minimum of intrusion within the surroundings. In 1994-5, United Artists installed cable television meaning that the town's roads and footpaths had to be dug up. In the event, this caused less disruption than originally feared.

Emergency services were another essential for the town. During 1968, residents were intrigued by the 70 ft tower being erected on the slopes of Craigshill, a feature which dominated the landscape for many years until joined by the chimney of St John's Hospital. This was the training and hose drying facility of the new fire station which when it opened had one tender with one full-time crew but the potential to expand to three tenders when demand justified it. In the early 1970s, Livingston got its own ambulance service when the 16 radio linked vehicles of the Scottish Ambulance Service's West Lothian depot moved from Bangour. The first policemen appeared on the beat of Craigshill in the late 1960s with a permanent police headquarters opening in 1981.

A TOWN DESIGNED FOR THE CAR

The original layout of Livingston, as articulated in the Master Plan, was based on the assumption that the town had to be designed round the car. Without being completely dominated by roads, the layout had to make it easy for residents and businesses both to move within the town, from home to work and shops, and to access the wider transport network of East Central Scotland. The latter was essential if Livingston was to achieve its envisaged role as a regional centre and as an economic growth point.

In designing the town's internal transport system, the planners were influenced by a number of external factors. Sir Colin Buchanan had recently published his major report on "Traffic in Towns" which predicted an almost exponential growth in car ownership and underlined the critical importance of designing transport systems which kept cars and pedestrians strictly apart. There was the recent example of Cumbernauld, the first new town in Britain to embrace this principle.

The town's road system was developed on a grid plan with what became Houstoun Road, Cousland Road, Almondvale Road and Bankton Road providing the main east-west axis and Livingston and Alderstone Roads the main north-south links within the town. District roads provided access from housing cul de sacs and loops to the main elements of the grid. Initially, the town's district roads joined the dual carriageways by grid separated junctions. When it became clear that the traffic densities as originally envisaged would not be achieved and capital budgets for roads were at the same time shrinking, the cheaper option of single carriageways with roundabouts was used, thus continuing to avoid the need for traffic lights.

Building the road system was an immense operation. Livingston Road was the first north-south element of the grid to be built. During periods in 1969 and 1970, the town was virtually cut off while flyovers were built to carry Livingston Road over the M8 which was then under construction. In 1972, the Almond Valley was spanned by the award winning bridge across the river. The Corporation decided to build the bridge high above the valley to avoid disturbing the natural landscape of the river's flood plain. With the completion of Livingston Road, a link was provided between the M8 and the A71, the main route between Edinburgh and North Ayrshire.

Livingston Road high over the Almond Valley was the first artery to link the north and south of the town.

Front Door Back Door
The Radburn system which Livingston adopted proved a source of puzzlement to some residents, who could not understand why their house had two front doors, one on to the pedestrian foot path and one on to the road.

The road building programme kept pace with the opening of new areas for housing or industry as well as linking them with the town centre. Occasionally adjustments had to be made such as the straightening out of the tortuous bends on some district roads and the changing of the one way system within the town centre to create a two way traffic flow in Almondvale with improved circulation and access to facilitate the development of Phase 2.

Plans for completing the town road system were increasingly frustrated in the 1980s by delays and cutbacks in Lothian Regional Council's road building programme. Edinburgh's outer city bypass was finally built although it meant continuing delays for Livingston's road building programme. In its last years, the Corporation obtained permission and funding from the Scottish Office to complete Alderstone Road and Houstoun Road as Lothian Regional Council did not have the available budget. Unfortunately, this additional scope could not be extended to the completion of Starlaw Road which is required to provide a full standard connection between Bathgate and Livingston town centre.

Within the town, the original principle of keeping people and traffic strictly apart proved a mixed blessing. Livingston was one of the UK's safest towns, with only one fatal road accident in the first eleven years of its existence. After the hazards of tenement life, many mothers appreciated the benefits of being able to send their children to school or out to play, without having to keep a constant eye on them.

The downside was security. Especially as landscaping matured, walking home in the evening along footpaths lined with bushes and through dark underpasses could be a threatening experience, resulting in campaigns for better lighting and pruning the trees. Like car owners the world over, residents also liked to be close to their cars, both for security and convenience.

The Radburn system was virtually abandoned in later Corporation and private housing estates, with the introduction of mixer courts and traffic calming to replace it. In later years, the Corporation was forced to acknowledge some people's preference to walk close to roads rather than on segregated footpaths, by providing road side paths and crossing places.

Unlike some English new towns, the Master Plan made no provision for separate routes for cyclists on the grounds that cycling was not popular in Scotland. Adult cyclists were expected to use district roads, and children, the footpaths. Although surveys in the 1970s confirmed that cycling was not a popular means of transport in the town, within the next decade, increasing awareness of its health and environmental benefits led to the passing of the unique Livingston Traffic Regulation Order 1985. This permitted cycling on all the town's footpaths except overbridges. As cycling became a more popular leisure pastime, long distance routes were created with the Edinburgh to Glasgow Cycleway being directed through the Almond and Lochshot Burn valleys.

WAITING FOR THE BUS

In 1962, Livingston was not entirely cut off from the world despite the demise of passenger trains six years previously. There was an hourly bus service from Livingston Station to Bathgate and a service to Edinburgh via Broxburn. A mile walk gave access to a 20 minute service to Glasgow along the A8.

Provision of bus services is an example of the Catch 22 that all new towns faced. Although the Corporation accepted the argument of the bus operator, Scottish Omnibuses, that it could only provide services when they became economically viable, staff also sympathised with the plight of residents. In the late 1960s, when shopping within the town was limited, there were only hourly services to Edinburgh or Bathgate and no link with nearby Linlithgow. Within the town, services were slow to get off the ground and until 1969 residents did not even have the protection of a bus shelter against the elements. No sooner were they up than the Council took them down again, owing to a dispute over the design.

Constant pressure from residents and the Corporation resulted in improvements in the early 1970s, following a survey of passengers' needs. An early morning express service to Glasgow was introduced to transport workers who were still employed in the city and a late night bus from Edinburgh to Craigshill allowed residents access to the night life of the city. At last, daily services to and from Bangour Hospital were introduced and in 1979, the town got its own bus station.

Arguments with service operators rumbled on. Many hopes were pinned on the findings of the major SCOTMAP survey conducted by Scottish Omnibuses in 1981 to review its routes but the timetables remained much the same. In general, Lothian Regional Council adopted a very positive attitude to the planning and subsidy of bus services within the town although this had to be pulled back with deregulation in the late 1980s. Deregulation brought a flurry of new services and the new railway helped but Livingston has yet to resolve its bus services, at least to its residents' satisfaction.

A RETURN TO EDINBURGH OR GLASGOW

Unlike many new towns, Livingston was fortunate in that it was bounded by not one but two railway lines, the Edinburgh Princes Street/Glasgow Central line to the South and the Edinburgh/Bathgate/Airdrie line to the North. The latter had been closed to passenger

Will the Bus Come? Will the Train Stop?
Livingston's strategic position within Central Scotland was a significant factor in its designation. Persuading the transport authorities of this, when the town's population was still relatively small, was a much harder battle. As Secretary of State, Malcolm Rifkind ushered in a "Return to Livingston".

Toronto and Canberra

Apart from international golfers at Deer Park, the exceptions to the local or Scottish flavour of Livingston's street names are Howden and Craigshill West which adopt the placenames of Canada and Australia respectively. This unusual departure was occasioned by a request from the UK Government in the late 60s to commemorate the Commonwealth in street naming, at a time when the emphasis of trade and culture was shifting from the Commonwealth to Europe

As part of the Livingston Festival celebrations of 1973, the Corporation produced a giant street plan, the first map of the new town marked with every street and public building. A decade later, the Corporation commissioned a high quality map of the town from Clyde Surveys which went on sale in 1982

---

traffic in 1956 although freight continued to use the line as far as Bathgate.

The problem was to get the trains to stop. Although the Master Plan reserved land for a new railway station, it was to be twenty years before Livingston South station was opened in 1984, providing an hourly service to Edinburgh and Glasgow. Only eighteen months later, passenger trains were re-introduced on the Edinburgh Bathgate line and the name, Livingston Station, ceased to be an anomaly.

The intervening years were marked by many meetings between the Corporation and British Rail and at least one appeal by the Chairman to the Secretary of State for Scotland. While the local MP, Tam Dalyell, led several campaigns in support of new rail services, the Corporation commissioned feasibility studies to demonstrate the viability of the lines. With only one Scottish line in profit in the 1970s and the imminent death of local railways in the face of the relentless advance of the car widely predicted, British Rail's executives were cautious if not sceptical.

Two events were finally to change their minds: the increasing popularity of Livingston as a commuting town and the willingness of Lothian Regional Council and the Corporation to assist with the costs of the new stations, with additional funding for the Edinburgh-Bathgate line coming from the European Regional Development Fund. In its first year of operation, this line carried half a million passengers, exceeding all expectations and justifying the Corporation's tenacity.

A SENSE OF PLACE

It is a cliche that new towns are a hazard to navigation. The Corporation has worked hard at providing the town with clear directions, through the naming of streets, clear signing and the design of visual symbols to act as landmarks. These have not only helped people to find their way around the town but have contributed towards the more intangible but all important creation of a sense of identity

The main town roads were named after nearby fields, farms or natural features while district roads took the old name of the area that they passed through followed by a compass bearing such as Knightsridge East. Roundabouts, the natural focal point for directions, were also given names. "Turn left at Lizzie Brice" entered the town's vocabulary.

Within each district, a specific theme was adopted with a common suffix such as Way or Avenue being adopted for all streets in the area. The names of individual streets within a theme were assigned in alphabetical order. Themes for housing areas ranged from Scottish glens and rivers to famous golfers and writers. Durward and Kenilworth Rise in Dedridge recalled the novels of Walter Scott whereas the Ways of Knightsridge East summoned up the clans such as Cameron and Stewart. Streets within industrial areas were named after famous Scottish inventors, scientists and entrepreneurs from Joseph Lister to Andrew Carnegie, whereas most office blocks took the name of a Scottish mountain range.

Art has been used to create a very different set of landmarks. In commissioning public art, the Corporation provided a unique opportunity for citizens to participate in the selection process and occasionally even in the creation of the new works. It also offered a significant source of patronage for young Scottish artists.

Art first came to Livingston when in the late 1960s, the Deputy Chairman W K Geddes. championed the cause of identifying an appropriate statue for the new Craigshill Shopping Mall. After initial attempts to persuade a sponsor to donate a suitable work failed, the Board decided to offer a small fee to a number of young Scottish sculptors to come up with ideas and a sculpture was installed.

The Livingston Arts Guild was formed in 1970 by a group of residents committed to the visual arts. The Guild proved a strong ally in early initiatives to enhance the town. In 1973, with Corporation support, it ran a competition inviting residents to come up with ideas for outdoor art in a park, on a courtyard gable and within an underpass. Some of the 40 suggestions were taken on board by the Corporation.

The Corporation and the Livingston Arts Guild then set about the task of preparing a strategy for "beautifying the town", leading to the appointment of one of Scotland's first town artists in 1974. In developing his role, Denis Barns, a young art teacher and artist from Fife, continued the Renaissance concept of the artist as an integral part of the building process. He also helped the local community to express its own artistic aspirations and talents. Bloom Farm had its stone sheep: Craigshill had its Wiggle. If Livingston had yet to win the battle for a railway station, at least it could have an underpass dedicated to the train.

Factories, gable ends, play areas and the town centre all provided scope for the creative talents of Denis Barns and his team, and of the artists whom he commissioned including Ian Hamilton Finlay,

"The role of the town artist is to see that many of the jarring edges of the new town are smoothed and rounded so that the environment is as pleasing as possible to the mind's eye."
Denis Barns, Livingston Town Artist

Snipe and Scaup
The best of Livingston's many bird habitats is around the Almond Ponds where the bright flash of a diving kingfisher may occasionally be glimpsed. In February the Ponds come into their own as one of the area's few expanses of water not to freeze over in cold weather with tufted duck, teal, pochard, mallard, goldeneye, red breasted merganser and scaup. Snipe have increased in numbers on Kirkton Campus while flocks of golden plover and lapwings fly over Houstoun.

William Tucker, George Garson and Andrew Mylius. Denis Barns proved so successful as Livingston's artist that he went on to establish a business Town Art & Design, in the town, which created urban sculptures and furniture to enhance many streets in Scotland and further afield.

In its final years, the Corporation gave much thought to the creation of landmark sculptures throughout the town. In 1995, residents contributed to the selection of two sculptures for Livingston Square and the Boulevard Roundabout by voting for their choice at an exhibition of entries from artists throughout Scotland. "The Community" by Charles Anderson makes a civic statement in the town's main square and "Windvane Family" by Philip Johnson adopts the imagery of the town's main elements from trees to technology. Some of the town's children spent the hot summer of that year helping five artists from Scotland and the USA to create sculptures for the town centre, following a Symposium held by the Corporation to increase public awareness of the art of stone sculpture.

In order to provide a distinctive answer to the traditional difficulties of steering round new towns, the Corporation commissioned David Wilson, the Perth artist, to create sculptures for four of its roundabouts.

Made out of stone and copper, "Dyke-Swarm", "NORgate", "Compass" and "Chrysalis" celebrate the harmony between the natural environment and high technology which the town has achieved.

A SENSE OF SPACE

From designation, Livingston Development Corporation acknowledged the blessing which the natural landscape conferred on the site and resolved to conserve and enhance this asset wherever possible. Among the Board's first acts were the seeking of a tree preservation order and the setting up of a nursery to ensure that young trees were strong enough for planting as soon as the first districts were ready to take them.

By 1965, the Corporation's Landscape and Forestry Department had planted 13,000 young trees to start the process of restocking woodlands which had in some cases suffered from lack of management over the previous decades and of creating screens between developed and undeveloped areas of the town. In 1973, Lord Elibank planted the 500,000th tree on the site of Patrick Murray's Physic Garden.

Livingston was also fortunate in inheriting the parkland surrounding Howden House and the wooded estate of the long vanished Livingston Place where traces of a few of Patrick Murray's exotic species survive in what is now Peel Park. Within the Howden policies, the Corporation created the town's first park, which not only provided the setting for the traditional Sunday walk but a backdrop to countless events and Festivals.

In addition to these district parks, over the years, several major parks or Greenways intersecting the town from east to west were laid out by the Corporation. To the north is Dechmont Law Park and to the south is the Murieston Water Greenway, forming a link between town and country. In 1973, the Almond Valley Greenway was extended through the centre of Livingston and in 1979, on to Howden Park and Livingston Village reaching the former open cast ponds in the final phase of development. The Greenway was linked to many of the town's districts by a network of paths along the tributaries of the Almond. In the early 1980s, extensive use was made of the Corporation managed Community Programmes to create paths, viewing platforms, picnic areas and beaches within the bends of the river

Although no worse than in any other town with a young population, vandalism could be disheartening, given the substantial investment made by the Corporation in the environment. During the late 1970s the Landscape and Forestry staff prepared six monthly reports to the Board on the problem. The report for the Summer of 1979 makes typical, if depressing, reading – 47 instances of graffiti, 19 broken slabs and walling, 18 gully gratings and manhole covers damaged, 40 water toby lids missing and 36 cases of litter dumping. Over the next winter, 40 shopping trolleys were fished out of the Almond. Even although murals were painted in some of the underpasses, they were soon covered over with more informal art forms. The Landscape and Forestry manager reported in desperation: "whatever is done to improve the damage, within a few hours it will be as bad as ever."

The most enduring problem was litter, with regular disagreements between the Corporation and West Lothian District Council as to whose responsibility it was to keep streets and paths clean and where the money was coming from. Any moves to clean up the town were further frustrated by the Board decision that there should be no positive publicity to tackle vandalism in case it damaged the town's image for incoming investors and that "the oxygen of publicity" might simply encourage the vandals.

More constructively, it was decided that the way forward lay with educating the next generation about the environment. In 1981, as part of a major environmental exhibition at the Howden Park Centre, the Scottish Wildlife Trust ran a schools competition for pupils to look at ways of improving their school grounds and local environment. The next year, the Corporation assisted the schools to implement their projects from tree planting to sculptures and vegetable gardens. The funds from a sponsored spring cleaning were ploughed back into the soil.

With funding support from the Countryside Commission for Scotland, now Scottish Natural Heritage, in 1988 a Countryside Ranger Service was

Howden Park from Almondvale

established, based at Livingston Mill, to build on this interest as well as providing an advisory service to other Corporation staff on the management, conservation and use of the countryside within the town. From 1991, its staff encouraged local primary schools to adopt and manage an area of local woodland. In a project which is unique in Scottish education, local pupils have mapped their own woodlands, prepared nature trails and planted new trees.

Throughout its lifetime, the Corporation took care not to displace the native population, whether fox or foxglove. Areas of natural wilderness such as the ponds of Dedridge and the birchwood plantations of Bellsquarry were identified and policies developed to manage them in such a way as to retain their wilderness character while enhancing specific habitats for wildlife. Occasionally, such as at Bellsquarry and Muirieston, there were conflicting views between the Corporation and local residents about the impact of proposed road works on mature woodlands. 1990 saw the completion of a botanical survey carried out by a MSC survey team under the supervision of the Countryside Ranger Service which revealed that the town had 430 species of flowering plant including several, such as the early marsh orchid, which are rare within the Lothians.

A similar audit of bird life to which residents contributed by reporting sightings of birds was carried out in 1991. This identified 108 different species, over half of which were confirmed to be breeding within the town's varied habitats. Since then, the town's natural life has been audited on an annual basis, with the help of local people and organisations such as the West Lothian Bird Club which the Countryside Ranger Service helped to establish.

13
ALMONDVALE – HEART OF THE TOWN

Establishing the heart of a greenfield new town is inevitably the hardest task of all. The centre only becomes viable when the town's population reaches the size where it can justify the investment. On the other hand, people are reluctant to move to or to stay long in a town without a functioning heart. For visitors, the town centre is the town. Without this reference point, they see only an unrelated collection of houses and factories, lacking coherence or common purpose. A centre is essential to a town not only for the vital services it provides but also for the sense of civic pride it instils in its citizens.

It was to take many years of patient endeavour on the part of Livingston Development Corporation, years of revised plans, dashed hopes, budget cuts and planning uncertainties before the towns' residents could say they were "going into town".

THE EARLY VISION

In the early days of planning the town when everything seemed possible, the Board and officials each had their individual ideas of what the town centre should look like and what it should contain. Of course, it must have the essentials of shopping, offices and a hospital, in short all the standard services and amenities of an established town. What about a University, an Underground, a Heliport or even an Ecumenical Cathedral? All these and more were suggested in those first debates.

One of the strongest elements of the 1963 Master Plan was its initial design concept for the town centre. It was to sit within the Almond valley forming a series of bridges between the residential developments to the north and south. It would be realised in four phases starting from the south east corner of what is now Howden Park, near to where the new hospital was to be situated. From there, it would progress from east to west in parallel with the phasing of the town as a whole.

Building complexes would be sensitively integrated within a landscape which would include lakes formed by damming the river. The new District Hospital was to be a multi-storey structure which, conveniently, would provide an ideal landmark visible on approaching the centre on the new regional spine road. The centre would, of course, be built on several levels, providing total separation between pedestrians and vehicles "Ramps, and staircases will

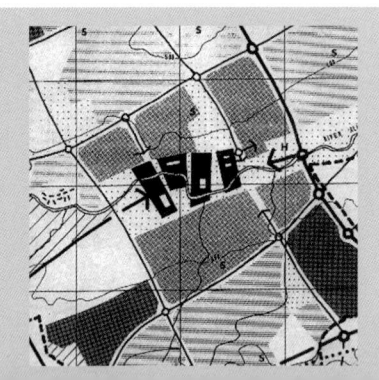

The 1963 Master Plan for the Town Centre
Ebeneezer Howard's vision that "society and nature should be enjoyed together. The two must be made one." was taken to heart by the planners when they conceived a town centre sitting astride the river and its floodplain.

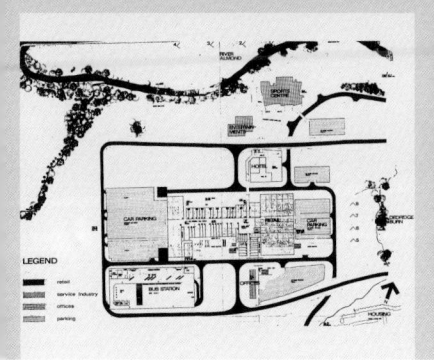

A Start to a Town Centre
Following local consultation, new towns were required to submit Stage A plans to the Secretary of State for Scotland outlining their proposals for a new area and the timescale for implementation. Almondvale 1 was built very much as planned.

lead to the pedestrian levels of the various sections of the central valley so that between these main elements, courts, piazzas, water areas, and changes of level may be designed."

The Master Plan map demonstrated these principles diagramatically with an informal configuration of four trapezoidal zones, together making a relatively compact area within the central section of the road grid. The report placed considerable emphasis on the importance of Almondvale's intended role as a regional centre in addition to serving the town. The road network was carefully designed to bring regional traffic directly into the centre from the surrounding area without becoming caught up in town traffic which would be carried on a separate system of roads.

THE FACTS OF LIFE

Unfortunately, the vision was soon confronted by reality, or by at least by the facts of life as they were seen at that time. When the engineers carried out test bores, they found that the buried pre-glacial bed of the river was well below the present surface, meaning that the depth of piling required to support the town centre structures would be inordinately expensive. There was also growing concern about the condition of the river and the risk of flooding.

Already in the 1966 revision to the Master Plan the river crossings were almost eliminated and the original, carefully tailored phases were lost in an amorphous single zone.

By 1967 the decision had been taken that the centre would be developed entirely on the south side of the river with the exception of the hospital. The proposed hospital was, therefore, moved to a much larger site in the north of Howden, thus becoming almost totally detached from the centre proper. In the detailed plans prepared at this time by the town centre team, however, the overall multi-level concept of the centre remained, now backed by a correspondingly complex road system. The two lochs were preserved but now situated within open parkland.

It was originally intended that the town centre infrastructure and the shopping development would be financed by the Corporation. The patience and enthusiasm of the team were sorely tried as discussions between the Corporation and the Scottish Development Department on the merits and viability, or otherwise, of the proposals dragged on until finally rejected in 1971. After initial dismay the staff were regrouped and the task of formulating a totally different planning and design concept was begun.

Following rejection of the proposal that the

Corporation should fund the retail element of the centre, the new concept had to take into account the need for a separate site, capable of being developed on a single level, if the developer so wished. The resulting "Livingston Regional Centre Stage A" report presented proposals based on a strong rectangular grid of distributor and service roads creating a series of island sites. These were connected by footpaths vertically segregated from the roads. This plan was approved by the Scottish Office within a few months of submission. Given the delays to date, the search for a developer was now an urgent priority and a number of companies were invited by the Corporation to submit designs and financial offers for the Phase 1 shopping development.

ALMONDVALE PHASE 1

The highest bid contained the bonus of a design which was very acceptable to the Corporation. The concept proposed by the major development company, Ravenseft Properties, was grander and more ambitious than the Corporation's brief had dared to hope. Ravenseft planned to create one of the largest indoor centres in the country. This incorporated what was then probably Scotland's largest superstore, a Woolco, which had been separately negotiated directly between the Corporation and Woolworths. The superstore would be located at the eastern end of a double shopping mall and beyond it Ravenseft proposed to build on the Corporation's behalf a dual multi-storey car park.

Once all the agreements were tied up, the Corporation quickly started work on the infrastructure for the centre, soon to be joined by Ravenseft and Woolco's contractors. Good progress was maintained and the Livingston Centre, as the developer chose to call it, opened to much rejoicing and even more relief in Autumn 1977 fifteen years after designation and at least 5 years later than the planners had intended. Although the somewhat bland exterior was not regarded with much favour, the shopping centre was a major success both with retailers and residents who when surveyed five years earlier had put "shopping" at the top of their list of dislikes about the town. The Centre also created the atmosphere of credibility that would encourage other facilities to follow suit. One shopper summed up the experience: "once you're in the Centre that's it. You're nice and dry and everything's to hand".

THE PICTURES OR THE DISCO?

The opening of the Centre had the hoped for effect

Christmas Shopping
The new shopping centre proved so popular that the Corporation had to provide 250 temporary car parking spaces to cope with the 1978 Christmas shopping rush. On the Saturday before Christmas, 7,500 cars were accommodated within the Almondvale Centre.

Largest Indoor Centre
A totally enclosed centre had both advantages and disadvantages. Good shelter in inclement weather but an anonymous exterior.

and over the next decade, other developers of town centre facilities followed Ravenseft's lead. The bus station opened in 1979, bringing to an end exposure to the elements on a bus stance amid the building site of the town centre to be. A cinema and bingo hall opened alongside the shopping centre and a discotec in Almondvale North provided a welcome alternative for the town's young people to the more formal youth centres and organised activities.

Despite the offer of free accommodation, it proved very difficult to persuade the local DHSS executives to open an office in the centre of town to save claimants having to travel to Bathgate. At a national level, however, Livingston triumphed as far back as 1973 in being selected as the first of three UK centres to run the new computerised local office system. Along with the first commercial offices, work started on the Divisional Police Headquarters in 1979. A social work office and an unemployment benefits office were opened in 1982 with a replacement for the temporary Job Centre opened in 1972.

Further elements fell into place during the 1980s: the Hilton National Hotel, an indoor bowling centre, the Icelandia six-sheet ice rink and a retail warehouse park. The local entrepreneur, David Murray, later to become Chairman of Rangers FC, made his first significant move into sports sponsorship by bringing a winning basketball team from Edinburgh to Livingston. It was for several years a very fruitful relationship. The Murray International Livingston Basketball team become UK champions in 1986 while their sponsor and the Corporation rewarded them with the Forum, a home base to be proud of. The Forum also provided the town with a venue for pop concerts and commercial entertainment.

ALMONDVALE PHASE 2

Although the shopping centre was now the largest by far in West Lothian it still lacked the identity, image and status compared with almost any other town of its size, much less one worthy of a sub-region. The Corporation was eager to build on this success. As early as 1978 it started to progress towards the second phase of retail and associated development. The general plan for the centre, extended to cover the entire central area, was submitted to the Scottish Office in 1979 and consultants were appointed to start on detailed designs. The "Almondvale Stage A" refined the previous layout concept, explored urban design issues within the centre and examined the potential for reducing dependence on multi-storey car parking which was proving highly unpopular with both shoppers and developers.

Initially, everything went well. The plan was approved by 1981 and good progress was made by the consultants. The Corporation, however, was experiencing difficulty in securing the private institutional funding it required to enable it to act as developer. While this situation remained unresolved, the first of a long succession of planning applications followed by public inquiries emerged for major free standing retail centres on the west side of Edinburgh. The Corporation was to spend almost the next ten years defending Almondvale's case against each proposal as it came forward.

While the Corporation was extremely successful in protecting Livingston's interests against these proposals, enormous damage was incurred in the form of continued delay to the Phase 2 proposals, as a result of retailer uncertainty caused by all the conflicting plans. Plans by the Heron Corporation for a Phase 2 development, accepted and given planning authorisation by the Corporation in 1989 languished as funding agencies took cold feet in the prevailing retail planning climate. The financial community may also have given the cold shoulder to Heron's Chairman Gerald Ronson, following in the wake of the Guinness scandal.

By the late 1980's it was clear that however or whenever Phase 2 of the shopping development was resolved, in the meantime it was necessary to review and revise many aspects of the town centre as a whole. The predominance of engineering structures, the introverted nature of the buildings and the often awkward arrangements for pedestrian circulation all contributed to the centre having a rather negative image. No doubt, this also contributed to the lack of enthusiasm by potential developers of Phase 2 and to adverse comments made by The Royal fine Art Commission for Scotland.

In preparing the "Almondvale Stage A part 2" report the Corporation engaged urban design consultants to recommend how the overall design of the centre could be improved and sought the advice of traffic calming experts on how to make the environment friendlier to both pedestrians and vehicles. The resulting proposals were to transform the whole character of the town centre. Approved by the Scottish Office in November 1992, detailed proposals for the Almondvale Boulevard and Livingston Square were quickly progressed, spurred on shortly by the Government's decision to bring forward the date of wind up of the Corporation.

After the withdrawal of the Heron Corporation, there was no option but to market the Phase 2 development opportunity once more from scratch.

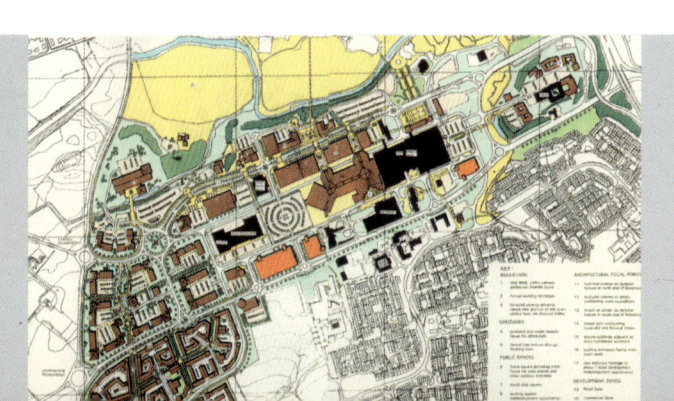

A Sign of Growing Confidence
The 1970s layout of Almondvale involved 17 bridges and 2.5 miles of roads. Implementing a comprehensive urban design strategy in the early 1990s transformed the area's character into a town centre.

The Much Awaited Almondvale 2
"Now, I'm proud rather than embarrassed when people ask me where the town centre is."
Livingston resident, 1996

This time, the marketing effort met with real success. Complementary proposals by the developers Amec and Safeway met the Corporation's requirement for a more open development and presence overlooking the new Boulevard. They also met the demands of the residents who by now were growing extremely restive about the lack of town shopping. The Safeway store was completed in Autumn 1995 and Phase 2 proper was opened on 17 August 1996 following strong interest in the three stores and 41 shop units available.

Ravenseft, now renamed Land Securities, the owners of Phase 1 of the centre had agreed to fund the development and to take it over on completion. The Phase 1 interior benefited from a major upgrading in 1992 and the improvement of the exterior has been carried out to coincide with the completion of Phase 2. Meanwhile, Asda who now occupy the original Woolco site, have proposals approved for a comprehensive upgrading of the interior and exterior of their store.

BEYOND PHASE 2

Including a planned major expansion to the retail warehouse complex, total shopping provision in Livingston will soon amount to over 800,000 sq ft. This places the town within sight of sub-regional status especially given the other key facilities and services in place or committed.

The Corporation has never been modest in its aspirations for the Centre. Its parting gesture has been to seek the additional, more specialist ingredients which will make sub-regional status beyond doubt. If these are realised, then both Livingston and West Lothian will have one of the most modern and attractive town centres in the country.

THE COMPLEXITIES OF LEISURE

Boredom and a lack of things to do in the evenings and at weekends was a common gripe of new town residents and Livingston was no exception. What most people in a predominantly young community wanted, centred on leisure sports such as swimming and indoor bowling. From the first, the Corporation set its heart on a major leisure centre to serve the whole town.

A working party was set up between the Corporation and the two County Councils to translate the vision into reality and a site was earmarked within the town centre. In the late 1960s, the Billingham Forum on Teesside was the most advanced sports and community centre in the UK. Following a visit to study its operation, senior officials decided that the Livingston resource should be modelled on

Billingham other than its community theatre. Estimated in the region of £1m, the cost would be shared equally by the three partners. The Corporation's contribution would come from its Major Amenity Fund. In 1962, the fund was set at £272,000 but this was topped up by £100,000 in 1973 in the light of inflation.

The ambitious project was not without its critics. The Rev Hamish Smith, one of the team ministers in the Ecumenical Experiment dismissed it as a white elephant and an example of the dichotomy between the planners and those that they planned for who were already struggling to raise finance for much more modest community resources. While acknowledging the difference in approach, the Corporation defended itself by pointing out that it had to cater not only for an existing population but for "the unknown incoming population of a whole town."

Joined by three of the District Councils of East Calder, Uphall and Livingston and Whitburn, in the early 1970s, the working group produced plans for a £600,000 sports facility to be built at the north east corner of the shopping centre. When the project was recosted, however, the final bill came to £2m causing growing unease among the local authorities. In a further revision, costs were readjusted to £1.7m and the final plans were published in 1973. The centre, a three storey building entered from the top, was to have a 25m main pool, with diving and toddlers' pools alongside, a sauna, a health studio, a sports hall, a cafe and squash courts.

The project was on the verge of going out to tender, when local government reorganisation intervened. The new Lothian Regional Council was beset by financial difficulties and many demands on its purse. Responsibility for recreation and leisure was initially split between Region and District making it difficult to secure commitment to such a major investment. While the larger plans remained on the stocks, albeit redesigned and on a different site, in 1979, Livingston got its first and much more modest indoor sports complex, and running track at Craigswood, with funding assistance from the Corporation.

In the early 1980s, following the Stodart Committee's report on how well the new system of local government was working, the decision was taken to move responsibility for recreation and leisure entirely to the District Councils but with little compensation in the way of financial resources. For a period in the wake of the British Leyland closure, West Lothian District Council's spending priorities were with Bathgate and their leisure priorities with the

Bubbles

Livingston Square, Livingston Town
In 1995, Livingston acquired a town square, fronted by the District Court and enhanced with sculpture including "The Community", a summing up of the creation of a town in thirty four years.

provision of small sports facilities in each community.

Like many local authorities, West Lothian believed that the coming trend was for leisure pools for family fun rather than swimming enthusiasts. Reluctantly, the Council and the Corporation agreed to a compromise in the provision of central swimming facilities. In 1993, the District Council opened its family leisure pool, Bubbles, the nearest that the town centre has yet achieved in its quest for a leisure centre, whereas the Corporation decided to use the remainder of its Major Amenity Fund to endow St Margaret's RC Secondary on the northern slope of the Almond Valley with a conventional swimming pool for clubs throughout the community.

A COLLEGE FOR THE TOWN

From the Master Plan onwards, it was always intended that the town should have a higher education facility. As well as being a hallmark of a major centre of population, this was seen as a critical training resource for companies moving to the town. It took over thirty years for Livingston to get close to achieving this aim.

Further education was provided in the town from 1969, with the setting up of a unit in Craigshill High School. Courses offered were largely geared to low level vocational qualifications and leisure. What the town needed and aspired to was a Technical College. Early in 1969, Midlothian County Council confirmed the goal but put back the timescale by two years.

The proposed College was to be built in three phases to match the growth of the town, with the first phase accommodating 420 students. Cutbacks in local government capital expenditure and the approaching reorganisation of local government introduced further delays.

By the early 1980s, West Lothian College was running out of space in Bathgate. Some classes moved to temporary accommodation in Brucefield Industrial Estate and James Young and Graigshill High Schools, raising expectations. In the Corporation's 1983 annual report, the Chairman noted that "the Corporation hopes that these classes will form the basis of an enlarged Further Education facility in the town in the future."

Over the 1980s and early 1990s, the College's presence in the town strengthened with the opening of facilities in Almondvale to provide a range of vocational training. A centre was opened on Kirkton Campus to train young people in the skills of the emerging discipline of mechatronics, the interface between mechanical and electronic engineering. A partnership of the College, the Corporation, local companies and Lothian and Edinburgh Enterprise backed this award winning training initiative which soon needed additional accommodation.

In the early 1990s, following a Government review of further education, West Lothian College, like its counterparts throughout Scotland, broke its local authority ties and became self-governing. It looked more and more to the new town as the market for its commercially orientated courses and as an opportunity to solve its accommodation crisis. In order to fund the development, the College planned to use the new Private Finance Initiative In 1996, the Corporation sold a site at the north west corner of the town centre to the College whose Board invited proposals from developers to design and build them a new West Lothian College. Whether Livingston finally achieves its hopes, first expressed as long ago as 1962, for an educational institution of regional or national stature, remains for the narrator of a future history of the town.

ADMINISTRATIVE CENTRE OF WEST LOTHIAN

A town hall is the official marker of civic status. In the early years, the possibility of Livingston seeking burgh status as several other Scottish new towns had done was raised on a number of occasions. The Provost of the SNP stronghold of Cumbernauld visited the town, using the issue of burgh status to try to drum up political support. Livingston residents, however, remained largely lukewarm. The strength of their civic voice had come initially from Forum and more recently from the Community Council. For whatever reason, few people were interested in a career in local politics and for much of its history, Livingston residents have been under represented as Councillors.

This was partly the reason why Livingston's hopes of becoming the administrative centre of West Lothian were set back in 1975 when the new District Council chose Bathgate rather than Livingston for its headquarters. At the time, Livingston's councillors were divided between the Labour party and the SNP weakening the effectiveness of lobbying for the new headquarters. Twenty years and another reorganisation of local government later, Livingston now has achieved the hoped for status with West Lothian Council in the centre of town and a new District Court gracing Livingston Square. From Forum to Council chamber, Livingston has come a long way in providing residents with a civic voice.

LIVINGSTON UNITED

Although historically, the heart of a town is the civic space at its centre, its pulse is often measured by the fortunes of its football team. One aspiration which did not form part of the early vision was that one day Livingston might have its own football team. In 1995, this was realised when Livingston FC, formerly Meadowbank Thistle, kicked off in an opening friendly match with Kilmarnock, in its own 4,000 seater stadium at the west end of the town centre.

Going for Goals
Its first season was auspicious. Livingston FC, West Lothian's first senior football team in modern times, moved from the bottom to the top of the Third Division. With match attendances increasing tenfold, an additional 1,800 seater stand was under construction as the team's first season in the Second Division opened. One day Livingston FC may join Livingston in the Premier League.

·NO LONGER A NEW TOWN·

·NEW TOWN TO HOME TOWN·

It was always envisaged that one day, British new towns would cease to be "new", reaching the position where they were able to take their place within the normal fabric of urban life. Nonetheless it came as a shock in the late 1970s when the Government announced the start of the process of what became known as wind-up. Arrangements were made to transfer the assets of the English and Welsh Development Corporations to the Commission of the New Towns. Housing was handed over to the local authorities and the Commission itself initially acted as industrial landlord although later policy required it to market its industrial property portfolio to the private sector.

The Scottish new towns were not included in the wind-up arrangements and for several years, their business continued as before. The harsher realities of economic life and the greater reliance on public sector investment may have influenced the decision, to allow a longer period to build investor confidence. In 1979, Livingston's original population targets were not even halfway to being met; the first phase of Almondvale was only recently open; NEC had only just announced its plans.

There was still much to be done and there seemed plenty of time in which to achieve it. Staff knew that one day, the Corporation would share a similar fate to the English and Welsh new towns. Nonetheless, it was difficult for anyone to envisage a time when "LDC" or "the Corporation" would no longer be landlord, employer, or sufferer from "the thorn in the flesh" of the community, as the Reverend James Maitland once described his role.

Livingston was the first Scottish new town to undertake a formal review of its Master Plan. The Corporation's decision to update its Plan was reinforced by the desire to defend its position against the young and ambitious Lothian Regional Council rather than by any premonitions of the future. Yet, it would be only four years before the Scottish Office requested all the new towns to update their development plans, spelling out what remained to be done.

MOVING CLOSER TO WIND-UP

At the start of the 1980s, change was in the air. The recession resulted in a painful industrial restructuring and the view that the way forward for the UK economy was to reduce inflation and dependence on the public purse. The radical policies of the Thatcher era encouraged the sale of public assets, from housing to transport, with the private sector expected to play a much more prominent role in infrastructure investment. Like all public bodies, the Corporation had to adapt rapidly to changed circumstances and priorities, although for its staff, used to working within a commercial environment, the change was less traumatic than for many of their public sector colleagues.

In 1981, the Scottish Office issued its Policy Statement on the New Towns. This acknowledged their outstanding achievements in attracting international investment and their pivotal role in economic growth. The smaller print, however, contained the first hint that irrevocable change was on the way. "When each new town has reached the stage of growth necessary to establish it as a viable, economic and social entity, within the physical framework provided in the designated area, then the purpose of the corporation will be fulfilled and the town can cease to be new." The Policy Statement stated, however, that wind-up would be triggered only when a town came close to 5,000 of its target population. Given the existing rate of population growth in Livingston, this was estimated to be realised in the early years of the next Millennium.

In 1982, the Secretary of State changed the formula for calculating the trigger date for the five year wind-up period, announcing that the process would begin when a specified percentage of each new town's target population had been reached. The exact percentage would vary depending on "the circumstances, prospects and unique characteristics of each town." He invited the New Town Corporations to prepare Development Profiles to establish how much investment was required for them to complete their programmes.

Following their submission in 1983, the Secretary of State published the new population levels at which wind-up would begin. In Livingston's case, this was 71% of the original target of 70,000. He reassured the Corporations that in no case, would this process start until the 1990s but given the uncertainties of economic and population forecasts, he reserved the right to reassess the situation in 1989.

During the latter half of the 1980s, the Corporation started to plan for the day when it might no longer exist. It invested many millions of pounds in renewing the housing stock and promoted greater diversity in types of house tenure. Tenants whether companies or residents were also encouraged to buy their property. New partnerships were formed with statutory and voluntary bodies. Projects with a reasonably short-time scale were completed without diverting energy from the longer term goals, notably of completing the town centre and of opening up the last areas for development.

At the end of 1988, after requesting updated Development Profiles from each Corporation, the Secretary of State issued "Maintaining the Momentum", a consultation document on the future of the new towns. For organisations, which had for so long been used to discussions on growth rather than simply maintaining momentum, this was a sign that the end was approaching. "Maintaining the Momentum" abandoned the concept of trigger populations, favouring instead a more general view of each town's maturity. The expectation was that the Corporations would be wound up during the 1990s in order of seniority, with a wind-up period of three years or less.

The document was a genuine exercise in consultation, welcomed by the Corporation and the ensuing debate was both lively and constructive. Many Corporation tenants participated in a national survey to establish their preferences on housing ownership. Like the tenants of the other three new towns surveyed, Livingston showed a preference for the District Council. Over twenty local organisations submitted their views on what should happen to their town, including Deans Community High School, Deans and District Labour Party and Deans Senior Citizens Club. Given the lower response to earlier local surveys and ballots, this showed that Livingston Station now saw itself as a member of the new town community.

The conclusions of the consultation exercise were drawn together in the Government's White Paper entitled "The Way Ahead", of July 1989. Designed to end uncertainties among staff, investors and residents, this made clear the timetable, if not how it was to be achieved. The wind-up of Livingston Development Corporation would commence in 1995 with final closure in 1998. The document proposed a number of options for the transfer of assets, including the formation of local development companies to carry forward the all important task of industrial promotion, and the management of community assets by local people. The final arrangements for housing were left open, to be decided at a later date.

Perhaps envisaging last minute pleas for extra time from the Corporations, "The Way Ahead" stated categorically that "only in the most exceptional circumstances" would the date for wind-up be changed. In 1992, these circumstances arose although not at the Corporation's request. With the recent creation of Local Enterprise Companies and the reorganisation of local government pending, the Government decided that it would be more sensible to adjust the timing of wind-up to coincide with the emergence of the new local authorities. As with designation thirty five years before, a Parliamentary Order was made to dissolve the Corporation on March 31st, 1997, with effective closure by the end of 1996. Despite vigorous protests from the Corporation, the Government's decision was final, although the allocation of an additional £70m to complete some of the outstanding tasks such as the roads network went some way to soften the blow if not the workload.

The Board and senior staff looked very seriously at the option of establishing a local development company as proposed in the legislation. In the end, the idea was rejected as it was difficult to see how it could be made to work in the new economic development environment. Instead, the Corporation set up an interim partnership, Invest in Lothian, with the aim of transferring the Corporation's longstanding experience of inward investment to Lothian and Edinburgh Enterprise Ltd. The future of other functions within the Corporation was shaped in different ways. The housing management team formed a new housing association through a management buy-out while the Landscape and Forestry Section became the Scottish arm of an international landscape firm. Some staff transferred to the new West Lothian Council, taking with them years of experience and expertise.

THE BUSIEST YEARS OF ITS LIFE

The Corporation's last years saw one of its greatest challenges, negotiating and implementing the transfer of its assets, including over £200m for sale, at a time when development activity was never greater and many of the town's employers including NEC, W L Gore and Shin-Etsu were in expansionist mood. Phase 2 of Almondvale was taking shape and the development of the later districts of Murieston and Eliburn was proceeding apace. Plans for the last

Almondvale Business Park
"The new town structure as a form of local administration as well as of urban development, provides an environment, backed with an administrative resource, which has shown itself to be eminently successful in the attraction of inward investment." **Policy Statement on the Scottish New Towns, Scottish Office, 1981.** *In total, the Corporation has made a capital investment of £419m in the town.*

Eliburn Goes Independent
Eliburn East was the first tenants co-operative in a Scottish new town, one of the initiatives encouraged by the Corporation to give people the greatest degree of choice in housing. It mirrored the Corporation's principle expressed in its housing renewal policy of 1984 "to equalise the quality of the housing stock so that no factor other than personal preference should influence tenants' choice of housing."

district, Adambrae, were well advanced. The interest shown in the town by developers and international companies helped to maintain staff morale through a difficult period.

A strategy for the disposal of assets was rapidly put together. Audits of everything from community centres to the town's wildlife were undertaken. The deed plans of properties were recorded using the new computer technique of Geographic Information Systems, resulting in Livingston having the most comprehensive set of GIS records of any Scottish town. Documents were archived for transfer to West Lothian Council. As it approved planning applications for over £200m of future development, the Corporation put its affairs in order for the day when its Special Development Order would be rescinded and planning authority transferred to West Lothian Council, in April 1996.

The Corporation had long since taken active steps in preparing its tenants for future change. A network of tenants associations was established in the late 1980s to ensure strong two way flows of information. For a number of years, housing associations had been active in the town and increasingly as houses became vacant, they were sold to the associations, in an arrangement known as trickle-transfer.

In 1994, four housing associations, Bield, Castle Rock, Edinvar and Almond, were invited to act as the Corporation's managing agents, for the two years before a ballot of tenants to choose their new landlord. The aim was to broaden their experience of management and thereby to inform their choice. Housing associations along with the local Council were then invited to bid for the housing assets on a district by district basis. The results of the ballot of tenants were announced in August, 1996 with formal transfer taking place a couple of months later. As in all the Scottish new towns, most of the ten districts voted to transfer to West Lothian Council. Two of the very first housing districts, however, Craigshill and Howden decided to stay with Almond Housing Association, the agency set up by the Corporation's own housing staff and residents of the town's sheltered accommodation voted strongly to remain with Bield.

The £100m industrial and commercial portfolio of land and buildings unsurprisingly attracted considerable interest from property developers and managers. By the time of wind-up, two thirds of the town's companies owned their own property with the active encouragement of the Corporation and

Brucefield Industrial Park was already in private ownership. Houstoun and parts of Deans Industrial Estate were sold in 1995, with Kirkton Campus following in the spring of 1996.

Over the past thirty years, the Corporation had acquired or created substantial environmental, civic and community assets, from the farms and Howden House to open spaces. Initially, it had been hoped to transfer some of these assets directly to the community but the revised wind-up timetable worked against the longer lead-times that such arrangements demand. The majority of these assets including Craigs Farm, and the Almond Valley Heritage Centre were transferred to West Lothian Council with a long lease to their respective Trusts along with land and some revenue earning properties to help pay for their future upkeep. The town's woodlands were largely handed over to The Woodland Trust with an endowment of £1.6m to ensure their continuing management and conservation.

In this way, the Corporation moved towards its end in an orderly and efficient manner and to its final headquarters on Brucefield Industrial Park. With a shrinking staff and the busiest town agenda of its lifespan, the remaining staff had little time to ponder or to debate what might have been.

Geology to Technology
One of the Corporation's last gestures sums up the town. "Dyke-Swarm" recalls the Five Sisters bings while the symbols of "The Windvane Family" bring together the elements of the town from nature to technology.

Newpark Roundabout

NORgate

· AN END AND A BEGINNING ·

Only a few weeks remain in the lifetime of the Corporation. As it once created "firsts", it is now time for the "lasts": the last site visit, Board meeting 447, the final farewells. Soon only the formalities of dissolution will remain to be accomplished between 1st January and 31st March, 1997.

In the Corporation's first annual report, the Board concluded by wishing "to place on record their appreciation of the magnitude of the task and the urgency with which it must be tackled". In 1996, Robert Watt ended his Chairman's introduction with the comment: "it is extremely satisfying to the Board that the original objectives set for the Corporation in 1962 have largely been achieved".

These objectives were twofold: to create a new focus of industrial activity in the Central Belt while acting as an economic magnet and centre for the immediate area of the Lothians, and to build 1,000 houses a year to cope with overspill from Glasgow. The former is the legacy which the Corporation has gifted to its town and the surrounding sub-region west of Edinburgh. Why the latter proved unrealistic is now part of history.

Inevitably, this short account has only touched on a few of the hopes, fears and triumphs of the intervening years. Setting out to create a new town was a bold endeavour, building it an immense undertaking and handing it over, as it is today, a remarkable achievement.

Looking back, Livingston, the Development Corporation and its partners have much to be proud of, from its track record in industrial promotion to its pioneering social experiments, now an established part of the town's way of life. Livingston has put down strong roots which draw from the past to nurture future growth.

Looking forward, the Corporation now hands over its tasks to its successors, confident that the town which it built has the resources to face the challenges of the future. What shape that future takes is in the hands of the citizens of Livingston.

In the coming century, Livingston is bound to face further changes, some of which will be dramatic in their impact if gradual in their onset. What would the shale miner employed by the Deans Oil Company in 1896 make of Livingston Station today, much less the farmer of 1796 bringing his grain to Livingston Mill? Whatever may happen, the town's greatest achievement and that of its Development Corporation is putting the name, Livingston, firmly on the map of the future.

121

·APPENDICES·

·LIVINGSTON DEVELOPMENT CORPORATION· ·BOARD MEMBERS AND DIRECTORS·

MEMBERS

Mrs S J Adamson	Member, 1972-76	M McSwan	Member, 1981-84
Mrs C Ballantine	Member, 1965-67	J Methven	Member, 1962-67
C A Boyle	Member, 1989-96	B A Meek	Deputy Chairman, 1987-96
J Boyle	Member, 1973-74	W J Miller	Member, 1962-67
Mrs I Brydie	Member, 1985-96	Dr B D Misselbrook	Chairman, 1972-78
W B Campbell	Member, 1989-91	Prof G S Milne	Member, 1993-96
J Clark	Member, 1978-80	R H S Muir	Member, 1987-92
T J Coleman	Member, 1985-92	W Pender	Member, 1970-75
M J Coyne	Member, 1975-86	W R V Percy	Deputy Chairman, 1983-86
W Connolly	Member, 1974-77		Member, 1986-96
Mrs V W Cunningham	Member, 1976-80	J B Rankin	Member, 1962-65
J Dick	Member, 1979-86	W G Rankine	Member, 1973-78
C Duggan	Member, 1967-75	A D Reid-Kay	Member, 1985-88
G R Gay	Member, 1967-82	Admiral Sir P Reid	Member, 1962-65
K Geddes	Member, 1993-95	Sir W Sinclair	Member, 1962-67
W K Geddes	Member, 1965-68	W Taylor	Deputy Chairman, 1962-65
	Deputy Chairman, 1968-79		Chairman, 1965-72
	Chairman, 1979-81	J Thomas	Member, 1995-96
W D H Gregson	Member, 1968-76	P Walker	Member, 1962-72
Mrs A H Hamilton	Member, 1975-84	W Walker	Member, 1976-84
I E Ivory	Member, 1992-96	T G Waterlow	Deputy Chairman, 1965-68
J Kelly	Member, 1967-73	R S Watt	Chairman, 1982-96
Sir D Lowe.	Chairman, 1962-65	Ms M Waugh	Member, 1967-72
D McCauley	Member, 1981-88	P Wilson	Deputy Chairman, 1979-82
		J S Young	Member, 1983-96

General Managers/Chief Executives *Brigadier Arthur Purches, S E M Wright, James Wilson, James Pollock*

DIRECTORS

D Balfour	Commercial Director, 1987-95	D F Kelly	Director of Property Services 1982-95
N C Bowman	Chief Engineer, 1984-88	J Kelly	Secretary and Legal Adviser, 1962-80
W Newman Brown	Chief Architect and Planning Officer 1966-82	A K Kinnear	Chief Finance Officer, 1976-90
A Dalton	Chief Finance Officer, 1962-76	G McPherson	Chief Estates Officer, 1969-78
P Daniel	Chief Architect and Planning Officer 1963-65	J Munro	Chief Engineer, 1969-84
G I Davies	Technical Director, 1982-96	D D Paterson	Chief Engineer 1963-69
E Donnelly	Director of Finance & Management Services 1990-96	J Pollock	Commercial Director 1978-87 Chief Executive, 1987-96
D Duncan	Director of Works 1989-91	Brigadier A Purches	General Manager, 1962-71
L Higgs	Housing and Social Relations Manager, 1964-82	J Ritchie	Secretary and Legal Adviser 1980-90
		J Wilson	Chief Executive, 1977-87
A Fletcher	Director of Works 1988-89	S E M Wright	General Manager, 1971-77

· CREDIT TO ·

The making of Livingston could not have been achieved without the commitment of the Development Corporation's many partners and liaison groups. Among the organisations who helped to make Livingston the town it is today were:

Aberlour Childcare Trust
Advisory Committee for Kirkton Campus
Almond Housing Association
Almond Valley Heritage Centre
Ark Housing Association
Bathgate Area Support for Enterprise (BASE)
Bathgate and Torphichen District Council
Bellsquarry Community Council
Bield Housing Association
British Airport Authority Consultative Committee for Edinburgh Airport
Carnegie UK Trust
Castle Rock Livingston
Central Scotland Countryside Trust
Children in Need
Citizens Advice Bureau
Committee on the Approach of the Churches to Livingston
Community Affairs Working Party
Countryside Commission for Scotland
Craigs Farm Community Development Project
Craigshill Initiative
Craigshill Leaking Flats Committee

Crime: Effective Action through Education
Dedridge Community Council
Dedridge Youth Council
East Calder District Council
East of Scotland Water
Edinburgh and Lothian Tourist Association/Board
Edinvar in Livingston Housing Association
Eliburn East Tenants Co-operative
Enable
European Commission
Films of Scotland Committee
Greater Livingston Growth Area Working Party
Hanover Housing Association
Health Services Joint Advisory Committee
Highways Working Party
Highlands & Islands Film Guild
Historic Scotland
Inter-Denominational Committee on Youth
Invest in Lothian
Joint Liaison Committees with Lothian Regional Council
Joint Livingston Committee of Churches
Joint Planning Advisory Committee
Kirk Care Housing Association
Knightsridge Community Council
Knightsridge Initiative
Knightsridge Youth Action Group
Licensing Planning Committee

Link Housing Association
Livingston & District Children's Fund
Livingston & District Council on Disability
Livingston & District Epilepsy Association
Livingston & District Festival Society
Livingston Action Committee on the Environment (LACE)
Livingston Action on Teenage Homelessness
Livingston and Whitburn District Council
Livingston Arts Guild
Livingston Christian Council
Livingston Community Affairs Liaison Group
Livingston Community Council
Livingston Community Project
Livingston Council of Churches
Livingston Ecumenical Council
Livingston Families Group Association
Livingston Federation of Residents and Tenants Associations
Livingston Industrial and Commercial Association (LICA)
Livingston International Sports Trust
Livingston International Youth Trust
Livingston Old People's Welfare Committee
Livingston Sports Council
Livingston Voluntary Organisations Council
Locate in Scotland
Lothian and Edinburgh Enterprise Ltd (LEEL)
Lothian European Affairs Forum
Lothian Health Board
Lothian Regional Council
Lothians and Peebles Executive Council
Lothians River Purification Board
Manpower Services Commission
Margaret Blackwood Housing Association
Marriage Guidance Bureau
Midlothian County Council
Open Door
Private House Builders Consultative Group
Provision for Youth Committee
Public Transport Working Party
Residents Action Committee 1972
Richmond Fellowship
Salvation Army
Save the Children Fund
Scotrail

Scottish Association for Mental Health
Scottish Bus Group
Scottish Council Development & Industry
Scottish Council for Social Services
Scottish Enterprise
Scottish Greenbelt Company
Scottish Homes
Scottish Housebuilders Federation
Scottish Local Authorities Special Housing Group
Scottish Natural Heritage
Scottish Office
Scottish Society for the Mentally Handicapped
Scottish Software Federation
Scottish Special Housing Association
Scottish Wildlife Trust
Social Workers Lunch Club
South East of Scotland Development Authority
South-Eastern Regional Hospital Board (Scotland)
SSMH (Homes)
The Woodland Trust
Training Agency
UK Carnegie Trust
Unemployed Voluntary Action Fund
Uphall District Council
View Point Housing Association
Voluntary Action West Lothian
West Lothian Business Alliance
West Lothian College
West Lothian Council
West Lothian County Council
West Lothian District Council
West Lothian Enterprise
West Lothian Hospitals Board of Management
West Lothian ITEC
West Lothian NHS Trust
West Lothian Project
West Lothian Town Twinning Association
West Lothian Working Party
West Lothian Youth Theatre
Wind-Up Consultative Forum
YMCA
YWCA

Thanks also go to the countless number of individuals - residents, business people, politicians, professionals and staff - without whom the making of Livingston would not have been possible.

BIBLIOGRAPHY

1991 Census Factsheet. Livingston Development Corporation, undated.

1991 Census Results for Livingston. Analysis of the Resident Labour Force. Livingston Development Corporation, undated.

1991 Census Results for Livingston. Livingston Development Corporation, undated.

The Anatomy of Scotland. Edited Linklater and Donniston. Chambers, 1992

Annual Reports 1986-96. Livingston Development Corporation, 1986-96

Annual Reports of the Cumbernauld, East Kilbride, Glenrothes, Irvine and Livingston Development Corporations for the Year Ended 31st March 1963-85. HMSO, 1963-85

The Best Laid Plans by Margaret Perry. Article in Town & Country Planning, March 1996.

The Buildings of Scotland: Lothian by Colin McWilliam. Penguin Books, 1978.

Central Scotland: A Programme for Development and Growth. Cmd 2188. Scottish Development Department. HMSO, 1963.

The City that Refused to Die: Glasgow, the Politics of Urban Regeneration by M Keating. Aberdeen University Press, 1983.

Consultative Document on the Scottish New Towns. Scottish Development Department, 1975

Disposal of New Town Assets. National Audit Office. HMSO, 1986.

Draft New Town (Livingston) Designation Order, 1962. HMSO, 1962

East Kilbride, Scotland's First New Town - A Benchmark of Urban Regeneration by James T Cameron. East Kilbride Development Corporation, 1996

Ebeneezer Howard: An Illustrated Life of Sir Ebeneezer Howard 1850-1928 by John Moss-Eccardt. Shire Publications, undated.

Economics and New Towns: A Comparative Study of the US, the UK and Australia by Albert J Robinson. Praeger Publishers, undated.

The Employment Performance of Established Manufacturing Industry on the Scottish New Towns by R A Henderson. ESU Discussion Paper No 16. Industry Department for Scotland, 1982.

Enjoy Your Retirement in Livingston: Livingston Development Corporation and Livingston Old People's Welfare Committee, 1971

Enterprise and New Towns (Scotland) Act 1990

Final Report of the New Towns Committee. Cmd 6876. HMSO, 1946.

The First Hundred Families. HMSO, 1965.

The Garden City Utopia, A critical Biography of Ebeneezer Howard by Robert Beevers. MacMillan, 1988.

Glasgow Going for a Song by Sean Damer. Lawrence and Wishart Ltd, 1990.

The History of Livingston by William F Hendrie. Livingston Development Corporation, 1988

James "Paraffin" Young, by John Butt. Scottish Men of Science Series, 1985

Livingston 25 Years. Livingston Development Corporation, 1987.

Livingston at Leisure: Community, Social, Recreational and Cultural Activities. Livingston Development Corporation, 1971

Livingston Botanical Atlas. Livingston Development Corporation, 1990.

Livingston Business Directory. Livingston Development Corporation, 1994

Livingston Community Guide. Livingston Development Corporation, 1995

Livingston Development Profile 1983. Livingston Development Corporation, 1983

Livingston Development Profile Review. Livingston Development Corporation, 1988

Livingston Household Survey 1972. Livingston Development Corporation, 1973

Livingston Household Survey 1977. Livingston Development Corporation, 1978

Livingston in Old Picture Postcards by William F Hendrie. European Library, 1987.

Livingston Local Plan. West Lothian District Council, 1995.

Livingston Master Plan Report. Livingston Development Corporation, 1963

Livingston Master Plan Review. Livingston Development Corporation, 1989

Livingston Plan. Livingston Development Corporation, June 1979.

Livingston PLC. Adam Smith Institute, 1988

The Livingston Post.

The Livingston Project: The First Five Years by Dr A H Duncan. Scottish Health Service Studies 29. Scottish Home and Health Department, 1973.

Livingston: A Town for the 21st Century. Livingston Development Corporation, 1995

Lothian Region Survey and Plan. Midlothian and West Lothian Joint Planning Advisory Committee and Scottish Development Department. Vols 1-2. HMSO, 1968.

Lothian Structure Plan. Lothian Regional Council, 1979 and revisions.

Maintaining the Momentum. Scottish Office, 1988

Make it in Livingston: the Accent's on Living. Livingston Development Corporation,. undated.

Memorials of His Time by Lord Cockburn. T N Foulis, 1910.

Minutes of Board Meetings. Livingston Development Corporation, 1962-1996

Murray's Handbook for Scotland. 1894.

New Life for Urban Scotland. HMSO, 1988.

The New Statistical Account of Scotland. Vol 2. William Blackwood and Sons, 1845.

New Town (Livingston) (Development Corporation) Order 1962. HMSO, 1962

New Town (Livingston) (Development Corporation) Wind-Up Order. HMSO, 1992

New Town (Livingston) Designation Amendment Order 1978. HMSO, 1978.

New Town Heritage: Glenrothes 1948-95 by Keith Ferguson, Glenrothes Development Corporation, 1996.

New Town, Home Town - the Lessons of Experience by Colin Ward. Calouste Gulbenkian Foundation, 1993.

New Town: Social Involvement in Livingston by Leslie Higgs. William MacLellan, 1977

New Towns (Scotland) Act, 1946.

New Towns (Scotland) Act, 1968

New Towns in Scotland: A Policy Statement. Scottish Economic Planning Department, 1981.

The New Towns of Strathclyde by U A Wannop in Strathclyde: Changing Horizons ed John Butt and George Gordon. Scottish Academic Press, 1985.

New Towns Today: All Grown Up. Supplement to Scotland on Sunday, June `9th 1994.

The New Towns: The Answer to Megalopolis by Frederic Osborn and Arnold Whittick. Leonard Hill, 1963

Opencast Working of Oil Shale at Livingston by J M Caldwell, J Stein and R Keddie. Oil Conference organised by the Institute of Petroleum 1950.

Planning and Development. Livingston Development Corporation, 1991

Planning Exchange New Towns Record Project, 1996

Planning New Town Growth in Livingston. Local Government Operational Research Unit. Royal Institute of Public Administration, 1972.

Pointer. Scottish Council Development & Industry.

A Regional Survey and Plan for Central and South-East Scotland. Report to the Central and South-East Scotland Regional Planning Advisory Committee by Sir Frank Mears. 1948.

Report on the Scottish Economy 1961: Committee of Inquiry into the Scottish Economy under the Chairmanship of J N Toothill. Scottish Council (Development & Industry) undated.

Review of the Master Plan. Draft for September Board. Internal document 11th August, 1966.

Scotland: the New Future by George T Murray. Scottish Television Ltd, 1973.

Sewage Treatment Works at East Calder and Newbridge. Official opening by the Rt Hon William Ross. 23rd September 1969. Midlothian County Council and West Lothian County Council, 1969.

The Scotsman.

Scottish New Towns: Analysis of Population, Employment and Housing 1973-93. Scottish Development Department, 1984.

The Scottish New Towns: the Way Ahead. Cm 711. HMSO, 1989

Scottish Townscape by Colin McWilliam. Collins, 1975.

Secretary of State for Scotland: Written Answer to Parliamentary Question 14th November, 1984. Hansard col 279-80.

Shale Oil: Scotland. David Kerr

Social Aspects of Planning in New Towns by H M Wirz. Saxon House/Lexington Books, 1975

The Statistical Account of Scotland. Vol 20. 1798

Survey of Scottish New Town Tenants. Scottish Office Central Research Unit, 1989.

The Third Statistical Account of Scotland: vol XX1 The County of West Lothian. Scottish Academic Press, 1992.

Town and Country Planning (Scotland) - (New Town of Livingston)(Special Development) Order. HMSO, 1962.

Town and Country Planning Journal

The West Lothian Courier.

West Lothian: An Illustrated Architectural Guide by Richard Jaques and Charles McKean. The Rutland Press, 1994.

What's in a Name: the Origin of Placenames. Livingston Development Corporation, undated.

What's On in Livingston. Livingston Development Corporation.

INDEX

Adambrae 32, 33
Alderstone 5
Aldous, Ron 83
Almond, River 3, 4, 5, 6
Almond Housing Association 66, 119
Almond Valley Heritage Centre 120
Almondvale 40, 56, 74, 92, 106-114, 118
Art, Public 102-103
Bankton 5
Barns, Denis 102-103
Bellsquarry 4, 6, 19, 105
Board Members and Directors 122
Brown, William Newman 43
Brucefield Industrial Park 53, 120
Bubbles Swimming Pool 113
Business and Industry 41-57
   Ashton Containers 46
   Brooklyns Westbrick 46
   B Sky B 49
   Burr - Brown 50
   Cameron Iron Works 26, 42, 43, 44, 46, 50
   Damon Biotech 52
   Digital Equipment 56
   EPS (Moulders) 46
   Ethicon Ltd (Arbrook) 49
   W. L. Gore 48, 118
   Inland Revenue 56
   Integrated Power Semiconductors 52-53
   Intelligent Applications Ltd 53
   John Laing 43, 59, 60
   Lee Cooper Jeans 46
   Mitsubishi 54
   Motec 51
   Motorola 53, 54
   NEC 2, 50, 54, 118
   Paterson 44
   Pringle Knitwear 46
   Pye - TMC 52
   Red House (Rooflights) Ltd 46
   Roneo Ltd 41
   Schlumberger 50
   Seagate Technology 53
   Shin - Etsu Handotai 50, 118
   Sperry - Univac 50, 52
   Surgikos 48
   Tulloch Engineering 46
   Unisys 52
   Wilson Byard 46
   Wyman Gordon 43
   Yale & Towne 43
Byrne, Father John 79
Charlesfield House 5
Clyde Valley Regional Plan 13, 14
Churches 72-73
   Carmondean 73
   Craigshill 72
   Lanthorn Centre 72, 80, 82
   St Andrew's 73, 78, 79
   St Columba's 73
   St Paul's 73
Community Councils (see also Forum) 1, 84, 86-87, 114
Countryside Ranger Service 103-104
Craigs Farm 78,81,82,87,120
Craigshill 30, 33, 37, 43, 56, 59, 60, 63, 64, 83, 85, 119
Craigshill Social Club 88
Cruickshank, Max 83

Dalton, Arnold 23
Daniel, Peter 23, 27, 28, 29, 48
Deans 1, 7, 32, 47, 50, 51, 60, 61, 66, 120
Deans Crude Oil Works 7, 19
Deans Institute 8, 19, 92
Dechmont Farm 80
Dechmont Law 4, 5
Dedridge 7, 60, 61, 105
Dedridge Youth Centre 84
Deer Park Golf Course and Country Club 75, 93
Draft New Town (Livingston) Designation Order 1962 20, 21, 22, 28, 29
Ecumenical Experiment 2, 72, 78-80
Eliburn 61
Eliburn Campus 32, 49
Fairways Business Park 50
Filipek, Paul 2
Forum 1, 78, 81, 86, 114
Garden Cities 10 ff, 30
Glasgow Overspill 15, 16, 20, 36-37, 41, 62
Hardy, Rev Brian 79
Harrysmuir Community Pavilion 82
Higgs, Leslie 64, 66, 77
Housing and Social Relations 63-64
Houston Industrial Estate 26, 42, 44, 47, 120
Howard, Ebenezer 10, 11, 12
Howden 1, 5, 60, 85, 119
Howden House 24, 89, 103
Howden Park Centre 33, 104
Icelandia 109
Inquiry into the Scottish Economy 1960-61 17
Jespersen system 43, 59, 60, 80
Johnson, Philip 103
Kelly, James 23, 24
Kirkton 1, 42, 48, 56, 57
Kirkton Campus 2, 31, 48, 49, 113, 120
Knightsridge 37, 60, 61, 63, 64, 66, 83, 85
Ladywell 37, 56, 60, 61
Landscape & Forestry Department 103-104, 118
Lauder House 56
de Leving 5
Livingston Arts Association 88, 102
Livingston Centre 39
Livingston Festival 77, 90-91
Livingston Garden Association 91
Livingston Industrial and Commercial Association 43
Livingston Life 85
Livingston Operatic Society 88
Livingston Place 5, 103
Livingston Plan 1979 33
Livingston Players 88
Livingston United Football Club 19, 114
Livingston Voluntary Organisations Council 40, 87, 91
Livingston Station 1, 4, 7, 8, 19, 24, 28 59, 77, 117
Livingston Village 1, 4, 6, 8, 18, 19, 24, 2, 6, 57, 66, 104
Locate in Scotland 51
Lothians Regional Survey and Plan 25, 27, 28, 29, 32, 40, 54
Lowe, Sir David 1, 23, 48
McGovern, Peter 27
Maintaining the Momentum 117
Maitland, Rev James 79, 80
Medical Services 71-72
Methven, James 23

Mews Theatre 88
Miller, William 23, 26
Mills 6
   Adam Robertson & Co Ltd 41
   Livingston Mill 6
   New Calder Mills 6
Mosswood Centre 82
Murray International Livingston Basketball Team 109
New Town (Livingston) (Development Corporation) Order 1962 22, 34, 36
New Towns (Scotland) Act 1946 12
Newyearfield 1, 5
Newyearfield Farm 82
Oakbank 7
Pumpherston Oil Co 7, 8
Paraffin Light & Mineral Oil Company 6
Parks 103-104
Peel House 56
Peel Park 5
Purches, Brigadier Arthur 13, 26, 28, 89
Rankine, John 23
Ravenseft Properties 108
Reid, Rear Admiral Sir Peter 23
Reith, Lord 11, 12, 77
St John's Hospital 72, 107
Schools 68-71
   Almondbank Primary 68, 70
   Craigshill High 39, 68, 69, 113
   Deans Primary 69
   Inveralmond Community High 69, 70
   Knightsridge Primary 69
   Letham Primary 68
   Riverside Primary 68, 70, 79, 83, 85
   St Andrew's R. C. Primary 70
   St. Margaret's Secondary 71
   Toronto Primary 69
   James Young High 71
Shale Mining 4, 6, 7, 18
Shiel House 56
Shops & Shopping 73-74, 106-114
   Almondvale 106-114
   Asda 111
   Carmondean 74
   Craigshill Shopping Mall 73, 74, 78
   Krazy Kuts 73
   Safeway 111
   Woolco 108
Sidlaw House 24, 57
Silicon Glen 49-50, 54
Sinclair, Sir William 23
Sport & Leisure 8, 19, 37, 75-76, 88-90, 92-93, 109, 111-112
Taylor, William 23, 74
Torrance, Rev David 79
Tower Restaurant 74, 78
Transport Systems 97-101
   Bus Services 30, 32, 40, 99-100
   Railway 7, 100-101
   Roads 101
Union Carbide 55
Walker, Peter 23
Watt, Robert 1, 121
Wilson, David 103
Wright, S.E.M 1
West Lothian Oil Co 7
West Lothian Youth Theatre 90
Young, James 6, 7

Livingston Development Corporation Board 1996
J Thomas, C A Boyle, I Brydie, W R V Percy, R S Watt, I E Ivory, B A Meek, J S Young, Prof G S Milne